Couples at Work

How Can You Stand To Work With Your Spouse?

E.W. and Janet James

Boomer House Books

Couples at Work
How Can You Stand To Work With Your Spouse?

By E.W. "Dub" and Janet James

Published by:

Boomer House Books
191 University Blvd., #323
Denver, Colorado 80206-4613
800-440-5402

First Edition

Library of Congress Catalog Card Number: 96-095182
ISBN: 0-9655804-9-0

CONTENTS

Introduction..13

Chapter 1: For Better And For Work.....................17

Who Wants To Do This Anyway?.............................19
Advantages Of Working Together.............................20
There Are Disadvantages... 21
Understanding Your Desire To Work Together..........24
What If Only One Of You Wants To Work Together?........26

Chapter 2: Partnering Agreements.......................33

How To Begin Working Together.............................35
Things That Go Into A Traditional Agreement..........38

Chapter 3: Divide And Conquer............................43

Is Defining Duties Important?..................................45
Who Does What?..46
Priorities Can Cause Problems................................48

Chapter 4: Who's The Boss?.................................55

Is It Important To Have A Boss 57
What If You Both Want To Be Boss?........................58
Some Businesses Require A "Boss".........................60
Some Thoughts About Titles....................................60

Chapter 5: The Invisible Woman...........................65

Must Women Roar?..69
Lighten Up Ladies..70
Capture Them With Confidence...............................73

Talk To Be Noticed..75
Men Can Help..77
Women Are Gaining Ground - Slowly But Surely............79

Chapter 6: Money Matters................................85

Same Money — Different View.............................87
Women Need Men...87
Men Need Women...89
Different Money Styles Can Dance.......................90
Resolving Your Money Differences......................91
What If You Just Can't Dance?............................95

Chapter 7: Making Management Music...........105

People Manage Differently.................................107
Personality Affects Management Styles...........107
He and She Differences....................................114
Couples at Work Have The Best of Both Worlds............115
Creating A Joint Style......................................116
Two Heads Are Better Than One........................121
The Temporary Rules.......................................121
When It Doesn't Work......................................123

Chapter 8: Cultivating Conflict.....................131

What Is This Things Called Conflict?.................134
Changing The Way You See Conflict..................135
Is It Possible To See Conflict As Good?.............137
How Should You Begin?....................................139
Fighting In Style...142
When Conflict Never Gets Resolved..................144

*Chapter 9: Getting Time Off - From Work and Each
Other*..151

Exactly How Important Is Time Off?.................152

Planning Your Time Off...154
Is That The Alarm?..158
Getting The Time You Need..159

Chapter 10: When It's Time To Say Goodbye...................177

How Do You Leave A Business?...................................178
When To Quit...180
When One of You Goes..181
If You Plan To Sell It...183
When You Plan To Pass It On..185
Shed A Few Tears..187

Chapter 11: Family Matters...191

Children Are Unique..193
Advantages Of Working With Your Children..................194
Disadvantages Of Working With Your Children..............196
When They Work With You...198
What If It Just Doesn't Work?..199

Chapter 12: Master Minding...205

Master Mind Your Way To Success...............................206

Thank you to our many survey respondents
whose contributions gave our own experience credibility.

Survey participants were solicited randomly from all over the United States. Respondents range in age groups from 20 to over 65 and represent a multitude of professions. They have worked and lived together from less than a year to over thirty years.

Each volunteer was asked to answer 23 questions with multiple choice answers and five essay questions. Those who had children were asked to respond to five more queries. Questions originated from the unavailability of specific information.

The generous response and honest outpouring of emotions and experience was touching. Many respondents chose to remain anonymous. Although their names are withheld, our sincere appreciation to them is not.

We salute all these couples who were willing to share their experiences. We applaud their perseverance to find better ways to mix personal relationships with business and we wish them all the adventure of being a Couple at Work.

Doug and Lily Vieyra, Eureka, CA., Sally and (Larry) Brownell, South Dartmouth, MA., Robert and Gloria Merkle, Honolulu, HI., Sally and Howard Krueger, Flagstaff, AZ., James and Leonora Metzger, Manasota, FL., Carolyn and Arnold Westwood, Windsor, MA., Margot Doohan, Stryker, MT., George and Cevia Rosol, Kittery, ME., Jerry and Mary Jane Campbell, San Francisco, CA., Jim and Ruth Boylan, Marshall, NC., Joy and Ray R. Still, Tillamook, OR., Doug and Rita Pruett, Pikeville, TN., Brenda and Ray Raffurty, Cape Cod, MA., Donald G. and Alma M. Swiers, Oakland, CA., Awanda and James D. Nowatzki, Jamestown, ND., Christian and Phyllis Baldenhofer, North Bay, CA., Vic and Barbara Mangini, Manchester, NH., Denise L. Sexton, Stockton, CA., Mike Bundgaard, Denver, CO., Diane and Friedrich M.

Rechberger, North Bay, CA., Gary M. and Phyllis J. Jones, Eureka Springs, AR., Robert L. and Donna Jean Siewert, Knoxville, TN., Tom and Mary DeHaven, Portland, OR., Wilhelmina and David Smith, Greensvoro, VT., Bud and Lee Raynor, San Gregorio, CA., Jimmy P. Leonard, Dothan, AL., Mary and Joe Shurilla, Canton, OH., Rob R. and Judy A. De Tar, Denver, CO., Peg Duffy, Valley Ford, CA., Sherry and Rob Shinn, Kansas City, MO., Jim and Linda McCarthy, Eugene, OR., Charlene and Paul Sloan, Denver, CO., Arch B. and Jane F. Edwards, Rocky Mount, NC., Janet and Stan Corneal, Key West, FL., Brian and Lisa Crawford, Honolulu, HI., Vera and David Steinfeld, Orlando, FL., Judy H. and Emil W. Milkey, Dillsboro, NC., David N. and Jean Panko Kaplan, Palatine, IL., Marshall and Vickie J. Ragle, Dallas, TX., Marjorie and John Pratt, Middlesex-Essex, MA., Charles Rosemann, Syracruse, NY., Mark and Joyce Erickson Pitts, Kalamazoo, MI., Kathy and Doug Larson, Salt Lake City, UT., Peter T. and Claudia W. Needham, Portsmouth, NH., Anita and Bobby Gill, Fayetteville, NC., Guenter K. and Kathleen Hubert, Newport, NH., Susan and Gerald Corsover, Plantation, FL., Leonard E. and Karen C. Weiss, Fort Lauderdale, FL., Bill and Millie Stinson, Burlington, VT., Tamela S. and Thomas Kenning, Ouray, CO., Glenn and Joy Hagen, Webster, SD., Charles Bulzone, Staten Island, NY., Donna and Robert C. Marriott, St. Augustine, FL., Bruce Holmes and Maryallen Estes, Asheville, NC., Sally and Edward Guishard, San Diego, CA., Debi C. and Robert J. Sutton, Jr., Harwood, MD., John H. and Beverly Grayson, Goodlettsville, TN., Jan and Doug Willbanks, Atherton, CA., Christy Lacey-Igoe, South Jersey, NJ., Elaine Dickson, Cape Cod, MA., Robert Bethel, Springfield, MO., Barbara Hahn, Sun Prairie, WI., Edward and Millicent Adams, Asheville, NC., Patricia M. Kelley, Milton, MA., Ellen Lassman, Long Island, NY., Robert A. LeGresley, Lawrence, KS., Mrs. Bernard Jaeger, Madison, WI., Marvin and Babette Henschel, Elkhorn, WI., J. Reed and Steven Robbins, Oakland, CA., William K. and Marilyn G. Sanko-Ebel, Lancaster, PA., Jr., Jacqueline and Larry Wolfe, Denver, CO., Bruce and Marcia McDougal, Davenport, CA., and Geraldine Moss.

Acknowledgment

To the many people who have supported us with interest, encouragement and advice, we offer our genuine gratitude.

A special thanks to the following who went the extra mile for us in a variety of ways:

Mike Shoenberger, whose enthusiasm for the project and periodic phone calls to check on our progress were nothing less than inspirational.

Colleen Murphy, Dawn Gardner, and Randy Johnson, of The Center For The New West and The Rocky Mountain Home-Based Business Association respectively, who encouraged us with their words and actions.

Patricia Frishkoff, Director, Austin Family Business Program, Oregon State University, whose interest and enthusiasm for couples that live and work together provided us with encouragement and possibilities.

Kirstin Marr, George Roche, and Bob Schram, who edited the book, developed the illustrations and designed the cover respectively, who walked us through the process and helped us meet our deadlines.

The core employees at Jamesville Office Furnishings, Dave, Mike, Scott, Jennifer, and the memory of Jim, who provided us with experiences to tell about.

All the editors and publishers around the country who voluntarily printed our notice in their publications to help solicit survey volunteers.

All our friends and family who supplied us with sources for the survey, especially *Susan Becker.*

Greg Gieseke, my son, who never stops believing in me.

Amy James, my daughter, who is part of all my lessons.

Scott Bradley, for that all important phone call.

Dedication

To Dub

Who knows what living an adventure is all about;
who continues to challenge me;
and who gave me the opportunity to be "three."

To Janet

Whom I searched for all my life;
who is my best friend, lover, wife, and partner;
and who shares my boundless thirst for life.

Foreword

Couples at Work are an unnoticed but emerging segment of the business market. In the past, this type of partnership generally evolved in a stereotypical pattern – the husband started an entrepreneurial venture and the wife stayed home to raise the family. She often kept the books for the business, because that task could be done between cooking meals and changing diapers, and because it didn't require her to be at the business on a fixed schedule. Plus, her husband was too busy with the day-to-day challenges of starting a company to do more than toss receipts and bills into a shoebox.

Today, couples are at work together because they want to be together and have chosen to develop their individual careers through a single entity – a business in which they share ownership – a family business. Two economic factors have significantly influenced the rapid growth of couple-owned businesses: (1) corporate downsizing and (2) the aging of America. Add to these factors the desire to have more balance between family and work life, and what emerges is the question raised by Dub and Janet James – *Can we stand to work together?*

Couples at Work don't fit any single demographic box. While

many couples are young, lots, especially those buying franchises, are retirees who can't imagine spending their days playing pinochle in a retirement center. Video production, nurseries, dry cleaners, coffee corners, high-tech manufacturers, computer repair services – whatever industry you name – couples are at work there. Their businesses are growing in small towns and large cities, in the United States and in the global marketplace.

The timing for this book is right. So is its approach – **celebrating Couples at Work**. This couple probably could have written a book called *Couples at War at Work*. Being in business together is a magnificent challenge; just ask any couple with experience. I applaud the authors for focusing on the magnificence, while having the good sense to integrate a strong dose of reality into each chapter. The press is already too focused on airing the drama of business-owning families in conflict.

Throughout the book, Dub and Janet share their own case story. These scenes make the book real. You'll feel like you know these folks and that they truly understand your situation. You may even wonder how they know so much about what happens between you and your spouse. That's because they've captured many themes common among couples. The simple illustrations raise powerful questions, with humor (always an important ingredient).

Because I want you to read this book, I'll only hint at some of its contents. The first piece of advice (bulleted in the book's format) convinced me that these authors were on the right track. What was that advice? – *sneak a kiss or hug on the job*. After all, isn't that what the marriage of love and business is all about?

Serious soul-searching is strongly recommended before embarking on being a Couple at Work. The authors detail the kinds of questions that should be discussed. I'd recommend writing down your answers. They recommend a formal partnering agreement, covering such expected contents as type of business and goals, and more personal issues such as how much you plan to work and who's going to take out the garbage. Their bulleted lists contain gems of advice; two especially good ones are the temporary rules for "making management music," and the distinctive principles shared by couples who have overcome the obstacles of conflicts in management style.

The book contains a whole chapter on time off – from work and from each other. Chapters are peppered with quotes from couples; most contain good advice, or raise critical questions. For example, Karen Weiss of Tamarac, Florida says, "Working together has strengthened our marriage." I would suggest that you ask each day – "How has working together strengthened our marriage today?"

I strongly recommend that you make this book your couples' handbook. To gain the greatest benefit, try this exercise: *Read the book together. Highlight those passages that seem really important to your situation. Then, when you want to celebrate or need to resolve a conflict, take it off the shelf as reference.*

Patricia A. Frishkoff, DBA
Director, Austin Family Business Program
Professor, College of Business

Oregon State University, Corvallis, OR

Introduction

This book is a celebration. It acknowledges a phenomenon of two people combining their individual spirits and energies and experiencing a new, third, sense of themselves. It is *for* couples who dream of working together, and it is *about* couples who have taken the leap and are living it everyday.

We are a couple who dreamt about it and now live it everyday. From as far back as we can remember and long before we met, we each thought that living and working with the one you love would make life complete. We thought that operating as a single unit would be romantic and practical at the same time.

When the time came to take the leap, it didn't look the way we imagined. The obstacle course we confronted forced us to struggle through narrow tunnels, climb rocky cliffs and argue about who got to lead the parade. In other words, it challenged us to experience our different and often opposite approaches to management, money, time off, and conflict.

What kept us going was a current of excitement. In spite of the turmoil, something was emerging; something we didn't plan intentionally. By becoming *one, we had become three.* By joining together we had not become a single unit, we had become you, I and *us*. The stronger this new existence became, the more we were inspired to find ways to remove the obstacles. The results were intoxicating and seductive. We felt exhilarated, unlimited and tireless.

Only in retrospect, did we discover the actions we unconsciously applied had enabled the creation of another self. We wondered if our progress and evolution would have been quicker and less painful had we been aware of the path we "accidentally" took.

Knowing what we do now, we write this book for you in hopes that you too can experience the magic of one plus one equals three. We are not experts. We are a "Couple at Work" who has something to share and hope that what we went through can encourage and support you.

This book asks you to give yourself the opportunity to experience life as it was meant to be an — adventure. It provides a road map for getting to know yourself, being open-minded and honestly examining your intentions, goals and dreams.

It's a book that challenges you to accept your partner on every level, to let go of judgmental habits and release behaviors that restrict you as a person and in your personal relationships. The only requirement is that you be *willing* and *ready* to receive the suggestions made.

Family businesses have been around forever. Millions of people throughout the world are still choosing to work together as couples. Many of them come from corporate backgrounds where jobs are insecure and life is controlled. Some have retired and started second careers. Still others are strictly entrepreneurs and wouldn't consider it any other way.

Today's brand of Couples at Work is educated, experienced

and expects equal and capable contributions from each other. They bring complimentary skills and make decisions together.

Working together as a couple is not for everyone. The subtitle of this book, "How Can You Stand To Work With Your Spouse?" reflects a reality for many people who prefer to keep career and personal relationships separate. These couples know themselves in this regard and more power to them for acting on that knowledge.

For the rest of us, an adventure awaits. Let's get started!

E.W." Dub" and Janet James

"This book was written by a REAL Couple at Work. It will help any couple. A MUST book for your Couple at Work library."
—Mike and Mary Shoenberger, Sacramento, CA

Chapter 1
For Better And For Work

Dub

The timing was bad. A few months earlier, I had suggested to her, for the umpteenth time, that we needed space. Now she was dating someone else and I had a growing sick feeling that he might be Mr. Right.

It had been a year and a half since I'd started the business. I had recently bought out my partner and hired my roommate, a needy but strong-willed personality to help fill in the gaps. He was a great salesman, but I needed someone I could trust to run the daily operation, oversee the employees and keep an eye on the checkbook.

With her management background and trustworthy nature, Janet was just the ticket. Unfortunately, for the past six years we had one of those on-again-off-again relationships. It had been love at first sight and we knew from the start that we were destined to be together, but after 15 years of bachelorhood, settling down was a scary prospect. From the beginning, we'd wanted to work together but things just kept getting in the way.

I never really felt I had anything to offer her until now. Although the business of resale office furniture wasn't the most glamorous, it had been in the black since opening day. For the first time since I'd met her I felt I had something of value to bring to the table.

I willingly proposed that she assume equal ownership of everything I owned (personal and business). All she had to do was quit her job, stop seeing the other guy, move and make a life with me.

I had, in my best male profile, used my commitment to the business to make the c-c-c-c-commitment to our relationship.

1 had no idea how that would all change.

Janet

*You want me to do **what?***

I knew when I met this man six years earlier that he was trouble. In the first place, he was much too good-looking. And secondly, I am always in control and with him I definitely was not. I knew I had to take at least ten percent of the blame for the roller coaster relationship we'd had. But as any single woman of the 90's will attest, it was HIM who wouldn't commit.

And now all of a sudden, he wanted me to go into business with him?

Not only was he asking me to join him in a business he'd started a year and a half earlier, but he was asking me to work in a warehouse! Not the ambience I was accustomed to. I had spent eight years working my way up the corporate ladder in some pretty nice environments and after that had a business of my own. I was used to being in charge and calling the shots!

*On the other hand, it was what I'd always dreamed of —
working with the person I loved. That idea had always intrigued me. It was so romantic.*

*A rational person would, without hesitation, say 'no, of course
not. You prove to me that you can be consistently in this relationship, that you can be there for me when I need you, that you
can meet all my requirements for a partner in life and then,
maybe, I'll consider such a drastic action.' But as I sort of eluded
to above, I'm not sure I was rational...I gave him my answer.*

'I'll need six weeks to think about this.'

Who Wants To Do This Anyway?

In a survey of over 200 Couples at Work, most say they were
mutually interested in working together.   Surprised? It's true
that the "outside" world has a great curiosity as to why or how
couples can do it. "We would kill each other," is a common
response to the idea.

But for many couples who have made the decision, they say
"we wouldn't have it any other way." Being together 24 hours
a day may sound like complete drudgery to some, but in our
survey the most stated reason for working together is "we get to
be together all the time."

To some it means creating a third "brain" by combining two
individual minds. It is experiencing a fresh new entity within a
relationship that lives and pulses on a separate circuit. It provides a new energy, and develops ideas, products, and lifestyles
that may otherwise have gone undiscovered.

> *"I am committed to bringing out all sorts of new
> dimensions in the relationship. If we develop
> them, the businesss can only benefit."*
> *Jan Willbanks, Atherton, CA*

19

the book *Working Together*, Frank and Sharan Barnett introduce the concept of "wegos" instead of egos. A wego combines two individual egos into a force that focuses on the relationship and the enterprise instead of one's self. They describe it as evolving from the confidence of each partner that "together they possess the individual capabilities to achieve their goals and the realization that without *ourselves*, the concept of *myself* is meaningless."

Advantages Of Working Together

> *"We get to be together all the time. Isn't that why we got married?"* A.U., Fairbanks, AK

Couples at Work who find inspiration in their situation find many perks in so much togetherness. Simple everyday pressures dissolve as they go about their day in sync. Such things as having to explain why you are working late or why you can't stay for breakfast are nonexistent.

If you want time off to support your children in an unfinished project, you won't worry about an explanation to the boss. Maybe you're having a dinner party and need the afternoon to finish it up — you can rearrange and prioritize your workload without asking anyone for permission. Judge for yourself some of the many benefits experienced by Couples at Work.

> *"It's great fun."* C.T., Naples, FL.

◆ **Sneak a kiss or hug on the job**. Laugh together about little situations as they occur or take an exercise class together at 10 a.m.

◆ **Share the peaks and valleys together.** Giving strength to each other during the bad times, and sharing the excitement when things are going well is exhilarating.

◆   *Enjoy a deeper appreciation for each other's talents and skills.* Having a partner that provides balance to your characteristics can be rewarding as well as efficient.

Most of us bring special characteristics to the work scene that are often invisible or inactive in our personal lives. It can be enlightening and refreshing to experience your partner in another dimension.

◆   *Notice qualities.* Some qualities may go undiscovered in other circumstances. Be aware of these in each other and help them unfold.

> *"My husband is my best friend and the person with whom I would most like to spend my time. We share ethical and aesthetic values that are 100% in sync — a rare pleasure."*
> P.B., Healdsburg, CA

◆   *Develop bonds.* Share common goals and dreams. Growing a business together is like raising a child. Your heart and soul are invested in the accomplishments and heartaches.

◆   *Experience the joys of team effort.* Successes are heightened and disappointments are softened with the loving company of another.

◆   *Indulge in the luxury of having a trustworthy sounding board.* Having someone listen in confidence, offer advice, perspective or support is a primary ingredient for fusion between two people.

There Are Disadvantages

Living with someone rarely equates to living in a perfect

world. Wonderful as it can be, daily conflicts, disagreements and mood swings are all part of the package. Having our brain cells arranged in a different order not only as individuals but as men and women, promotes many bumps and grinds along our journey together. Working together is no different.

> *"It's tough and I don't recommend it — it takes an emotionally mature couple to pull it off."*
> M.D., Bigfork, MT

◆ *New challenges can be unpleasant:* Instead of having only personal differences to negotiate, a new, often unfamiliar side of your partner may present a whole new challenge.

Although more often than not, working together seems to expand understanding of each other and serves as a building block to a more intimate relationship, sometimes it is shocking and unattractive to view your partner in this new role.

◆ *It can be stifling:* Some say instead of creating a new energy they are stifled by being together all the time. A psychotherapist and family-business consultant in Boston says that couples who work together have a difficult time becoming independent and growing as individuals.

> *"We're together so much I've lost my sense of independence."* M.D., Oregon City, OR

◆ *You may lose yourself:* Others would argue that instead of creating a third entity, you blend into one. When you mix yin and yang, you eliminate both. Much depends on your personal make-up and priorities.

◆ *You may lose romance:* Separating business and personal life can be difficult. Seeing too much of each other can kill the romance. Long hours can deplete you of energy and make you too tired for sex.

- ◆   ***Your styles may cause conflicts:*** If your management styles or personalities are in such opposition that you do not compliment each other, a great deal of work will be required to learn how to handle a business together.

You may want to reconsider your decision to work together. If you are a detriment to each other, you may well be a detriment to your business. Knowing yourselves and your personal make-up is an important key in weighing the pros and cons of working together.

> *"The greatest disadvantage of working together is that there is no place to hide or retreat when tensions arise!"*
> *A.W., Boise, ID*

- ◆   ***Your personal needs may not be met:*** Having no personal space or time is a common complaint among couples who work together. Making an intentional effort to respect individual needs is important.

- ◆   ***It can be risky:*** Working out of the same pot can be risky. There is usually no guaranteed monthly income, especially in the beginning. If your nature or circumstances do not allow for the risk involved, you will want to give serious consideration to your decision.

It is not unusual for couples as they first begin working together, to go through the trauma of sorting out their positions within the new framework. With a sincere dedication, love and respect for each other, the differences usually settle into a mutual and natural order and are often used as assets to benefit the company and the relationship.

Understanding Your Desire To Work Together

The only way to achieve the goal of "us" is to understand why you want to work together. Assessing and understanding your motivation for working with your life-mate frees both of you from the possibility of hidden agendas, misunderstandings and disappointments. It also gives you an edge when you are planning for the future. The more honest you can be about your intentions, whatever they are, the better chance you have of cultivating trust and respect.

Although our survey indicated that most Couples at Work work together by mutual desire, that is not to say they have the same reasons for doing so. Many times subtle assumptions are made on both sides causing hurt feelings or animosity later on.

Your business may be successful if you skip this step, but this is about more than business. It is about creating something new from the two of you that will enhance your relationship and your business. Unclear intentions is one of the few obstacles that is *easy* to avoid. Why overlook it?

> *"You need to know yourself and your partner pretty well before getting into the business together." G.D., Knoxville, TN*

Ask yourself why you want to work with your spouse. Do you:

♦   ***See life driven primarily by work and career?*** Do you think this may be the only way to truly share life at its fullest?

♦   ***Respect your partner's abilities*** and want to benefit from them?

♦   ***Need someone to control*** and think your mate is that someone?

♦ *Need a trustworthy partner* and view your partner as the best person to meet this need?

♦ *Want a gopher* and need someone to do the dirty little chores, lighten your load or fill in the gaps?

♦ *Need the personality, clout, money, or status* of your partner?

♦ *Not want to hire someone else* — want your partner to work for "free"?

♦ *Feel it is your spouse's responsibility* to work with you?

♦ *Like sharing all experiences*; don't like going it alone in any case?

♦ *See it as an opportunity* to enhance your relationship?

♦ *Want to re-create dynamic experiences* you had together in the past that were fueled by combining your energies?

♦ *See it as your only option?*

♦ *Feel it is economically wise?*

♦ *Want the professionalism* that your two personalities would create?

♦ *Feel sorry* because your partner lost a job, can't find work, or needs something to do?

What If Only One Of You Wants To Work Together?

Preferably you are working together because you both want to and because you are both qualified. Having both parties interested and enthusiastic in the business is the best chance for success.

But as our survey suggests, often the decision is made because it is economically correct. Sometimes this leaves one or both of you disgruntled, disappointed and unfulfilled. Before committing you or your partner to an unwanted position, try to find out why there is resistance. Do you or your partner:

◆ *Feel unqualified?* Often feelings of insecurity or inadequacy are founded on a misinterpretation of what is expected. Have the duties been clearly identified? If so, is some type of training available?

◆ *Dislike the business content?* We aspire to different mediums. While some like colorful, creative worlds filled with lots of people, others are at ease working with numbers in a solitary space. Is there an aspect of the business that can offer the elements desired?

◆ *Worry about what will happen to your relationship if you are together so intently?* Frank discussions and genuine appreciation combined with a commitment to openly discuss grievances and concerns as they occur may clear the air. Talking to other couples in similar situations can help define the obstacles and open a forum for finding solutions.

◆ *Have concerns about how your family life will be affected?* Some couples use family life as a reason to go into business together. They feel it gives them flexibility that they otherwise would not have. The best approach is to discuss ahead of time how you plan to manage family activities.

♦   ***Prefer to keep work and family separate?*** For some, having a distinctive family life without the complexities of work is important and refreshing. Is there a way to accomplish this if you are working together?

♦   ***Have an ambition unrelated to the business?*** Some enjoy having individual pursuits. Acknowledging each other's dreams and how they can be fulfilled is essential.

♦   ***Fear losing something?*** Apprehensions about loss of control, individuality or freedom are sometimes mistakenly connected with commitment. Talk it out with your partner.

♦   ***Afraid of the unknown?*** Not knowing what to expect or what is expected of you can be unnerving. A discussion about as many details about your expectations ahead of time clears up many concerns.

If soul searching has not made working together any more appealing, then it is time to consider alternatives. Although sometimes resistance can change into support and enthusiasm, more often than not an unwilling union does more harm than good to a business and a relationship.

> *"Two people with very strong opinions should not try to work together. BOTH must be willing to give. Couples MUST compliment each other — not compete." Lily Vieyra, Eureka, CA*

Try finding another partner. Although this might seem a

complex approach, it has the potential to work. Look for some-one to offset your own strengths and weaknesses. An outside partner may bring unanticipated expertise and financing to the table.

Hire someone to fill the position you hoped to be occupied by your mate. If your budget is tight, consider temporary help or a student who may need work credits. Do you have another family member who would be willing to pick up the slack?

Life being what it is, sometimes we do things out of neces-sity. Clearly, since many couples are motivated to work together for economical reasons, there are various situations where alternate solutions are not considered an option. This is not to say these couples do not enjoy working together; it is just to say they may have chosen to do something else had it seemed financially feasible.

If you find yourself one of those couples who cannot con-sider alternatives, acknowledge the position, be loving and respect the unwilling partner's involvement. Show apprecia-tion and support of each other and make every effort to see that both of your needs are met. Be flexible in your thinking.

◆ Can the work be done at home or on a part-time basis?

◆ Can a time-line or financial goal be established to sig-nify an end to the situation?

◆ Can a full-time work schedule be reduced to part-time?

◆ How can the hesitant partner be assured that his/her dreams are not abandoned?

Recognition, understanding and a genuine concern for each other's goals will go a long way in making the situation work. To insist on interest, energy and commitment to a business that holds no excitement to a person is futile and will probably destroy any vestige of support offered.

Dub

Six weeks!!

I couldn't imagine it! What would take her so long to decide? Isn't this what she always wanted? Now here it is. Either you want to or you don't (I didn't tell her that).

My mind was racing. I needed her NOW and what if I had to wait six weeks and she said 'no.' Then where am I?

I didn't think it was something you could hire just anyone to do. It required an all-consuming commitment to do what I wanted and needed and Janet was the only one I knew who would give me that.

Anyway this was what we'd been dreaming about for years. It was my first (of many) lessons in patience.

Janet

Within four weeks I was very clear. I didn't know if it would work or not and more time wasn't going to make any difference.

What I did know is that he had started this business with literally no money, little experience in the resale furniture market, and was somehow managing to pay an enormous monthly overhead. I also knew he was stressed to the limit and I wanted to help.

But most importantly, I knew that he was reaching out to me in the only way he knew to make a commitment. Because I loved him, I knew this was the chance I had to show him that being committed wasn't all that bad a deal. And if I was wrong, well, so be it; we could both move on.

I said I would give it a year and a half and then we'd see. I pulled out my handy notebook, positioned myself in the hammock and said, 'OK, what do you see me doing?' I got my answer. 'Everything I do,' he said. We had a contract.

*I guess you could say I did it for love. I found out later that you better do it **with** love, because you are going to be tested in every imaginable way. And I was.*

The first day on the job, I knew I had made a big mistake.

More Reading About Couples And Business

Aronoff, Craig and Ward, John L., *Rules for Nepotism,* Nation's Business, January 1993.

Caggiano, Christopher, *Married...With Companies,* Inc; May 1995.

Hurley, Dan, *Working Together, Living Together,* Woman's Day, May 1993.

Naisbitt, John and Aburdene, Patricia, *Megatrends 2000,* William Morrow and Company, Inc., 1990.

Nelton, Sharon, *Challenge Your Fundamental Assumptions,* Nation's Business, January 1993.

Peters, Thomas J. and Waterman Jr., Robert H., *In Search of Excellence,* Warner Books, 1984.

Popcorn, Faith, *The Popcorn Report,* Doubleday, 1992.

Tifft, Susan E., *How Does a Wife Work with Her Husband? Carefully,* Glamour, August 1995.

Survey responses to the question "Which MOST expresses your motivation for working together?"

"We were buying the business as a common lifestyle change."
Joyce Erickson Pitts, Union Pier, MI

"The store was a way for us to reach common goals."
Kathleen Hubert, Newport. NH

Chapter 2
Partnering Agreements

Dub

Janet's first day on the job was met with mixed reviews. Some saw her as a great looking woman and an opportunity to take advantage, while others saw her as the person taking over their job.

Some of the perceptions were right and some were not. The office manger was convinced that her place was history just as soon as Janet learned the books and the computer system (wrong). One of the salesman, who had become a self-imagined partner, saw his post disappearing by forced surrender to a woman (right).

The other salesperson accepted her as a good looking addition to the office and did not perceive her as a problem (right). The warehouse staff saw her as an attractive, but unenlightened ornament who didn't know the first thing about warehousing or office furniture, thereby making their job more fun (temporarily right, but permanently wrong). I saw her as someone I could dump all the stuff I hated to do and get on the road (right and wrong).

Making the announcement that she was "the boss," because she would be signing the checks and running the operation, stuck like fresh-out-of-the-package, dry spaghetti to the wall.

Janet

I arrived at the shop the way I was accustomed to arriving in the work environment — in a dress skirt, silk blouse and high heels. Everyone was very nice. But, like me, no one knew exactly what I was doing there. The office manager and one of the salesman thought I had come to take over their jobs, and the warehousemen knew better, but couldn't imagine what I would be doing.

Dub introduced me to everyone, showed me my cubicle next to his, opened his drawer, pulled out a bunch of files and said, 'you handle these now.' I had my job description. Feeling miserable and inadequate, I took a walk around to see what was going on.

Like many small businesses that grow quickly, chaos prevailed. There were two buildings. The first was divided into three sections: the front with a nice showroom and offices, the middle a second showroom with furniture stacked two layers deep, and the back was an area with racking filled with a variety of panel systems, parts, more furniture, etc.

Across a parking lot was the other building, called "the warehouse." It was piled high with...more stuff. I couldn't walk through it without catching my clothes on something and getting dirty.

All the employees seemed to be doing their own thing, making their own rules, setting their own hours. For the most part, they seemed happy although there was an air of confusion and uncertainty. The warehousemen were taking orders from the salesmen, the salesmen were making up their own rules as they went along, orders were going out incomplete, customers were complaining, and a lawsuit was in progress.

In the past, my career specialty had included going into branches of banks on the brink of disaster and turning them into superior audits. This scene of disorder was not new to me. I knew what to do and how much stress would be caused by the unpleasant nature of the things I had to do to turn this place around. After my last resurrection I'd vowed never to do it again. What was I doing here?

How To Begin Working Together

This is not a book about how to run a business. But there is one business practice that very much affects every partnership and especially one that involves Couples at Work. Developing a partnership agreement at the beginning of your working relationship is one more step towards making your joint undertaking a success.

"Do we really need a formal partnership agreement? Why bother with the paperwork if honesty, good faith, and trust are what really matter? Can't we just work on a handshake (or in the case of Couples at Work, a hug)?" Clifford and Warren in the *Partnership Book* respond to this commonly asked question:

"Our answer goes something like this: We'd like life to be so utopian that nothing is ever needed to be written out, but we've learned that effective business relationships depend in large measure on good planning and attention to detail.

Writing a common sense partnership agreement is definitely part of this process, if for no other reason than it's a better way to record an understanding than the all too fallible human memory.

Also, it should go without saying that there is so much in any business venture that cannot be foreseen that it makes obvious sense to try to anticipate what you can and reduce it to writing."

If your business organization is a partnership, then you will need to have a formal agreement for such things as opening a bank account. If you have another form of business, a partnership agreement may not be required, but for a couple it can serve as a valuable tool for clarifying your individual and joint perspectives.

> *"The primary objective should be 'discuss all issues.' The problem is that you don't know what the issues will be. If they could be defined — then addressed - written and signed — conflict might be lessened."*
> *F.T., Pensacola, FL*

Just because you are romantically involved with someone does not mean you have the same mind. In fact, couples often have very different interpretations. Anything you do to forewarn each other about your expectations and desires will increase your position of respect and loyalty.

Most of us don't like unpleasant surprises, especially when they interfere with our own personal needs and goals. Another benefit of writing down your thoughts is that it forces you to clarify to yourself what you expect.

Even if you've been working together for 10 years, it is not too late to develop an agreement. Or, if you already have one, to revise it. Although a partnership agreement is a document that can spare grief if things go wrong, it can also help you gain perspective of what you think and expect of each other.

> *" What we expected of each other was assumed — we knew each other's abilities."*
> *Donna Jean Siewert, Loudon, TN*

It is true that some couples are so in sync that writing a formal agreement seems silly and superfluous. For those of you in this category, consider that it could further confirm that indeed you think alike. Another benefit is recording where you started, how you imagined things in the beginning. Not infrequently, as time progresses and things change, so do our intentions and visions.

> *"After about a week of Jerry being at the inn full time I found myself irritated when he'd sit down to read the paper when there was still work to do. I said 'I'm calling a board of director's meeting.' He said 'Oh-oh, what did I do?'And I explained that if we were going to do the business together and be partners, there were no male or female jobs. If he wasn't busy and there were things to be done, do them. He's great now."* Mary Jane Campbell, Geyersville, CA

In some cases, it is easier to get momentum on the agreement after working together for awhile, especially if this is your first time. A few months on the job brings into focus exactly what needs to be done and who is best at doing what.

Start somewhere. At least have a conversation. If you don't like the words "partnership agreement", call it something else. Call it "What I Think and What You Think," "List of Expectations," "Our Vision," or whatever. The important thing is that you each know what the other is thinking and if you don't agree, you have an opportunity to express your viewpoint up front. If you still don't agree, you will be aware of it from the beginning.

Things That Go Into A Traditional Agreement

Traditional agreements cover a full range of topics. Although these are the technical aspects of a business venture, Couples at Work will be faced with at least some of them. Sources available to guide you through the process of completing a partnership agreement include books, small business development centers, business counselors, firms, and entrepreneurial centers at many universities. Software packages devised for business plan development often include sections on partnership agreements.

For general discussion, suggestions of items commonly addressed follow.

- Term of the partnership: are both partners committed to the same schedule (life, limited, indefinite, until certain goals are reached)
- How the partnership is funded
- What type of business will be conducted
- Personal business goals of the partners and the partnership
- Distribution of profits and compensation
- Duties of partners
- How unresolved disputes will be handled
- Sale or assignment of a partnership interest
- Continuing business if a partner withdraws, dies, becomes disabled, or retires
- Determining value of departing partner's interest
- Ending a business or partnership

Although the following can be found in a traditional agreement, Couples at Work should pay particular attention and dedication to finding consensus and/or understanding. Don't worry if you don't have all the answers. Just thinking about them will start the process of defining your position.

- ***Are you equal partners?*** What is equal? Money? Time?

Ownership? Responsibilities? Position?

◆ *How do you visualize your business?* What is the blue-print — a small local shop, many locations, a national chain? Do you want to get it up and running success-fully and then sell it, or get a manager while you take off and do something else or start another store?

◆ *How much time do you plan to spend working?* How much time do you expect your partner to spend working?

◆ *What about compensation?* Are you going to take sala-ries, whatever is left over at the end of the month, expenses only? Is this a temporary arrangement?

◆ *Will your profits be reinvested back into the business?* For how long? What will signify a change in this arrangement?

◆ *How will you handle your personal chores?* Who will do the shopping, laundry, housecleaning, meal prepa-ration.

◆ *How will you maintain a healthy family life?* What about your children? Who will pick them up from school, attend their functions, help them with their homework? Can they come to work with you?

◆ *Do you expect your social life to be affected by your* work schedule? If so, how?

◆ *Will your family and friends understand?* If you are unable to maintain your usual level of involvement with them, should you talk to them about it?

> "I'm sorry we did not think about communicating
> our expectations because in the first two years
> we nearly killed each other. We were really
> stressed to the limit."
> Christy Lacey-Igoe, Cape May, NJ

Penciling out your strategies and expectations has a magical effect on relationships. It creates a measure of intimacy and safety. It promotes confidence and stability in your partner and your future. And though decisions and agreements are not set in stone, they give direction and a sense of purpose.

Dub

The office manager soon realized her job was secure. After four weeks the roommate was history; the other salesman took the changes in stride and the warehousemen went about their day unaware of what was in store.

Me? I went on the road immediately and, when I came back, would make mid-course corrections — whatever Janet had done, I would 'fix.' (Wrong).

Many of our problems in the beginning would have been short-lived or non-existent if we had sat down and discussed our strengths and weaknesses, ideas on management, job descriptions, exit plan, etc...in other words, if we had a partnership agreement.

Janet

Dub and I were lucky that things worked out the way they did. Had we stayed in the business longer any number of things could have occurred that may have thrown us into a tizzy. Had one of us died, walked out from frustration or been suddenly called away, the other would have been left in a lurch with no agreement to guide us through a division or separation.

An agreement would also have eliminated, or at least eased, many of the problems that we faced in the start-up.

For example, what exactly did he expect me to do?

More Reading About Working Together

Clifford and Warner, *The Partnership Book,* Nolo Press, 1986.
Haman, Edward A., *How to Write Your Own Partnership Agreement,* Sphinx Publications, 1993.
Milano, Carol, *Couples Inc.,* Essence, June 1993.
Ward, John L. and Aronoff, Craig E., *Two "Laws" for Family Business,* Nation's Business, February 1993.

Survey responses *to the questions "What did you expect your partner's role in the business to be when you began working together, and did you communicate these expectations?"*

> "Not as clearly as we should have."
> H.H., Vancouver, WA

> "We didn't 'contract' these expectations, but it seemed to be a given." M. D., Stryker, MT

> "It's sort of an understood thing for us that we are partners in everything in our marriage."
> Peg Duffy, Valley Ford, CA

> We were 'Babes in the Woods,' and didn't know anything about B & B's, so we didn't have any expectations."
> Elaine Dickson, Cape Cod, MA

Chapter 3
Divide And Conquer

Dub

*I thought she would be a dynamo; come in, hire, fire and generate some order. Nothing seemed any different. No big changes, nobody acting any differently, no increase in sales, nothing. I kept asking myself 'What is she **doing**?' I needed a system in place and I needed it YESTERDAY! All I heard was 'soon'.*

I knew I was organized and had a good company. Sure there were some problems, but after a year and a half the company was growing and still in the black. Things were OK and I expected her to get a handle on the weak points and correct them.

It's true she had a lot to learn. She knew nothing about the business of resale office furniture, how the books were set-up or how a warehouse functions. She also needed to develop a pick-up and receiving system, sales plan, marketing program, and understand the expectations of our customer base. And she needed to get on the phone and find product!

Finally, one afternoon when she was going on and on about writing job descriptions or something, I'd heard enough. I told her she had to start locating furniture, because if we didn't get any soon, there would be no business.

That went over like a lead balloon...

Janet

In my usual style, I spent the next few weeks assessing things. Experience had taught me to make changes slowly. In this case, even if I'd wanted to jump in and revamp everything, I didn't know enough about the business to make much difference. Not to mention that I had no credibility with the employees.

With Dub taking over the buying function, he went on the road almost immediately. I was on my own, trying to be cheerful and pretend that I knew what I was doing. While everyone was polite and friendly, no one paid much attention to me.

It soon became obvious that the employees needed attention. Not only did they need direction and guidelines, they needed encouragement and discipline. Challenging as this always was to me, it gave me a sense of purpose. It was my bailiwick and I knew what to do.

I got rid of my high heels and began writing detailed job descriptions. The more I wrote, the more I learned. I covered every function, spoke to everyone about every moment of their day. Soon the business began to make sense. I began to see the possibilities. My engines were charged. I couldn't write fast enough.

One Sunday afternoon soon after I began this phase, Dub and I were sitting in the park discussing the business. I was sharing my growing excitement. He didn't seem involved in my conversation.

His thoughts were about getting quality furniture on the floor. He wanted me to get on the phone to companies around the state and find furniture. This, he said, was the life blood of the business. I was furious. Of course I knew it was important but wasn't that his job? And how dare he undermine my progress and ORDER me to undertake such a lowly task.

My resentment was growing...

Is Defining Duties Important?

In the last chapter, topics and advantages of a partnership agreement were discussed. Even more important is the specific assignment and definition of each task required to manage the successful operation of your company.

This is the nitty gritty, the down and dirty of the everyday obligations. It is here that things can quickly and drastically go askew, where misunderstandings, hurt feelings, and resentments can brew and destroy relationships and progress.

Of the couples in our survey, 88% said they talked to their partners about what they expected. A very good thing, too, because a whopping 47% said they expected a "what-ever-it-takes-week" to make the business a success.

Being clear about what you expect from each other and how that corresponds to your business activities is paramount. Assuming you know what your duties are is dangerous for both of you. Not only do you risk the possibility of being wrong, but important details may fall through the cracks.

"You've got to talk to each other." G.P., Flint, MI

> *"He is the cook and I leave it to him. I do the paperwork which he doesn't like."*
> D.R. Guerneville, CA

Some jobs may seem obvious, but in a business, there are too many things that have no particular definition. Even worse, uncertainty is an excellent tactic for creating tension and insecurity. This is not positive energy for a business partner, especially when your partner is your life mate.

Who Does What?

Dividing the responsibilities often falls naturally. If you are working together because of your complimentary qualities, it is easy to categorize many functions of a business. But in many cases, it is not so clear how to distribute the duties. Sometimes Couples at Work have similar strengths and weaknesses.

Whatever the case, it is important not to *assume* what your partner's contribution will be. You need each other working at full capacity, so be in agreement and understanding of the tasks you accept.

> *"Think out all the responsibilities of your own business and go ahead with both eyes fully open. Talk everything over in detail with your partner."* M.S., Waitsfield, VT

Separate your business structure into its basic components. Listed below are some of the associated functions contained in most businesses.

- ◆ **Sales & Marketing:** Meetings, tracking, advertising, networking, research, publicity, events, telecommunications, trade shows, product placement, and visibility

- ◆ **Customer Service:** Negotiating, developing rapport,

handling complaints, and follow-up

◆ ***Purchasing:*** Ordering supplies and equipment

◆ ***Buying:*** Attending shows, viewing product, negotiating deals, tracking inventory, studying trends and ordering product

◆ ***Operations:*** Developing procedures, maintaining equipment, coordinating personnel, customer demands, sales, marketing, purchasing, and planning

◆ ***Personnel:*** Meetings, salary administration, performance planning and development, evaluations, discipline, and motivation and rewards

◆ ***Accounting:*** Bookkeeping, reports, taxes, and budgeting

◆ ***Clerical:*** Correspondence, reports, reception, and tracking

◆ ***Maintenance:*** Janitorial and housekeeping

◆ ***Warehousing:*** Managing inventory, operating heavy equipment and filling orders

Using the list above as a base, evaluate yourselves by defining how the following factors affect your suitability for the various requirements of your particular business.

◆ ***Personality:*** What are your natural reactions to the situations encountered in your business? For a better understanding of your unique characteristics, turn to Chapter 7 and rate your personality traits on a scale of 0-3.

By understanding yourself, you will gain a better perspective of your differences and similarities as a couple and how they affect your responses to personal and professional activities.

♦   *Education:* You may have the qualities to do a particular job, but you may not have the training or know-how to move toward the result that you want. In some cases, acting on your gut feeling is enough, but in others it isn't. For example, some people have natural sales skills; training may stifle or interrupt their success. For others, a sales training program can serve to develop skills through awareness of how to use them.

♦   *Skills:* Who knows the techniques or processes required for successful marketing, buying, people management, and product development?

♦   *Desire*: You may have the personality, skills, and education to perform functions in your business but no interest in acting on them. A common example is people who have strong people-skills, plenty of training and experience supervising, have achieved excellent results but have exhausted all enthusiasm for it.

In assessing and distributing the requirements of your business, carefully weigh all factors that contribute to your success and *fulfillment.* When situations or duties arise that neither of you are suited for, make every effort to find alternatives. Plan to eliminate the task, hire someone else to do it, out-source it, or share it. Knowing an unpleasant job is temporary goes a long way in making it mentally manageable.

Priorities Can Cause Problems

Responsibilities go beyond job descriptions. Prioritizing

projects can also be misinterpreted by partners. If your idea of what you should be doing is different from that of your partner, you probably have a glitch in communication and/or perception.

It could be something as simple as waiting for an article from your partner so you can complete a brochure. You have an appointment with the printer at 11:30; at 11:15 you find your partner still on the phone prospecting for new clients. He believes what he is doing is appropriate and you are furious that you may be late for the appointment. What went wrong? Why isn't he writing the article?

Or it can be a complex, long-term issue. Maybe you are embarking on a program emphasizing employee development while your partner is planning to focus all your resources on a powerful marketing campaign. Why are you going off in different directions? Have you shared your concerns, ideas and desires?

> *"Don't force your mate to do a task he is not good at only because you refuse to do it. Hire someone so you can blame that person!"*
> *F.K. , Everett, WA*

Another reason couples sometimes interpret their priorities differently is that one or the other feels inadequate, unqualified or finds a job distasteful. The spontaneous reaction to a disagreeable task is avoidance.

The best anecdote to deal with these situations is to confront them and decide if something can be done.

◆　　Can someone else do the job?

Small companies are sprouting up all over the country to out-source jobs for other companies. Bookkeeping,

49

marketing and personnel management are just a few examples of services offered.

◆ Is it feasible to shift the workload to the more qualified partner?

◆ Is training available from within the company or from an outside source such as a seminar, class or home study course?

Training is available on a multitude of topics through many outlets including adult education, private learning centers, and business schools. Family Centers around the country offer valuable education and support specifically designed for family businesses.

> "At work we have separate roles and duties but are willing to 'lend a hand' to the other one to finish a chore more quickly."
> M.D., Oregon City, OR

If you are regularly sharing and discussing where your business is going, what you need to do to get there and breaking your strategies into monthly, weekly and daily assignments, your chances of working at odds with each other are greatly reduced.

Dub

I really did appreciate the progress Janet was making, but my concerns were growing. The inventory was getting low and I had visions of having a fine-tuned machine out of gas.

As the buyer now, I wanted to change the image of the company and bring in upscale quality furniture. At this point, the best way I knew to find it was to make mass phone calls and screen those who said they had what we needed. It was a time consuming process. I couldn't do it and be on the road at the same time.

Janet came up with a plan that worked for all of us. She developed a telemarketing program that worked well and could be assigned to a part-time employee with minimal supervision.

Janet

Being the strong willed person that I am, and believing that employees are a company's greatest asset, I did not give up my quest to develop an employee manual.

However, I was acutely aware that the business was balancing on a delicate wire and that Dub needed help in securing furniture. There was no one else to do the job, so I decided to give one hour a day to 'phoning for furniture' until I could come up with a better plan. It worked.

My calls brought in enough prospects to keep him busy viewing and bidding and I still had time to continue developing the manual and running the daily operation.

Of course this cooperation fueled a growing confusion about who had the last word...

More Reading About Couples And Business

Aronoff, Craig and Ward, John L., *Defining Your Family Business,* Nation's Business, May 1994.

Arterburn, Stephen, *Winning at Work Without Losing at Love,*T. Nelson Publishing, 1995.

Blumstein, Philip and Schwartz, Pepper, *American Couples,*William Morrow, 1983.

Coleman, Paul, *The 30 Secrets of Happily Married Couples,*Bob Adams, 1992.

Survey Responses *to the question "What MOST expresses your motivation for working together?"*

> " We were convinced that our skills used in prior work environments would make this work. A.Q., White Plains, NY

> "The business needed both of us. We have different skills." B.B., Bay City, MA

> "A move to Napa Valley and my inability to find employment in my professional career." Alma Swiers, Calistoga, CA

> "We had both worked for another corporation. We wanted to own our own business and be out of the corporate scene." A.M. Jamestown, N.D.

Survey responses *to the question "Are you willing to do 'whatever-it-takes' to make your business succeed?"*

"I think I am but he isn't, and that has
caused friction."
P.B., Healdsburg, CA

"As long as it works in our marriage."
Peg Duffy, Valley Ford, CA

"In the beginning I was. Now that we are
successful beyond expectations,
I'm not too sure."
Alma M. Swiers, Calistoga, CA

"I was. Now I'm making the
business fit my needs."
E.N., Fargo, ND

Chapter 4
Who's The Boss?

Dub

I liked being on the road. My days were full and productive. Sometimes I would leave Sacramento at 5 a.m., view product in San Francisco, Walnut Creek, Lafayette, and San Jose and be back at the shop by 4:30 p.m. It became a game; how many places could I get to and still make it back before the store closed.

I didn't want to lose touch with the operation. I had birthed the company, raised the people, developed our system and quite frankly it was hard to let go. Everyday when I returned I liked to employees and connect with the customers.

The truth is, I wanted to do everything and I didn't feel sure Janet was getting the job done. Six weeks had gone by and I couldn't see much difference. Of course, the plus was that I knew I could trust her and I didn't have to worry about where the money went or if product disappeared out the back door.

The critical day occurred one afternoon when I was doing my usual trek through the warehouse and noticed a growing sense of disorder. Instead of getting better the mess was multi-plying. I noticed inventory being pulled off racking and resting on precious floor space. I demanded to know what was going her.

Her reaction was stunning . Why was SHE upset?

Janet

Things were rolling. With the job descriptions almost done, I was starting to feel more confident about how things worked, the uncooperative salesman had been fired, and the furniture was coming in regularly. Things were still a mess, but I could feel that changes were eminent. I was ready to attack.

I wasn't quite sure where to start. With furniture coming in almost every day, we needed space to show it, store it, and price it. The warehouse was a disaster. The previous buyer had bought anything and everything from pizza ovens to executive desks. There were parts and pieces to panel systems in every nook and cranny and although everyone 'seemed' to know what we had, no one knew for sure, nor did they know exactly where it was or how much we had.

My inclination was to donate it all to a worthy cause — the dumpster. It's always easier to start with a clean slate. But I had a hunch that idea wouldn't fly. So I decided instead to rearrange it. In my mind, organization means having like things in the same area. But initially, it gets worse before it gets better.

It was my first real approach to the warehousemen. Not without reason, they had about as much respect for my warehouse experience as I did for theirs in motherhood. However, they nodded their heads up and down and said 'no problem' to my suggestion that we were going to move things around. I carefully explained how it would be a slow process and that we would do it one step at time.

Later that day, Dub returned from his road trip and, as was his custom, took a walk through the buildings to orient himself to the day's activities. When he got to the warehouse — and since I did not tell him what I was doing — he had a fit at the sight of the reorganization.

His knee-jerk reaction was to yell at the warehousemen 'What do you think you're doing? Who told you to put that there?!'

Their answer? 'Janet did.'

His response? 'Well, put it back!'

Six weeks had gone by; I began to reconsider my commitment to a year and a half...

Is It Important To Have A Boss?

The answer, of course, is yes and no. Yes, as it relates to employees and customers needing a mediator, a decision maker, a sounding board. No, because as in most things, it is a decision each couple has to make.

A title can automatically imply that one is the boss, i.e. CEO, President and Owner. Sometimes a title is just that, a title with no special control attached. In some cases one partner *needs* to be boss more than the other.

> *"I've always wanted to own my own business and also be the boss."*
> *P.B., Healdsburg, CA*

Maybe one of you spends more time in the business and it is only natural to be in charge. Or maybe one of you dislikes the responsibility of being the ultimate authority. Perhaps you each have areas of expertise and feel more secure having the last word in that area. The important thing is to be consistent with your decision, especially if you have employees.

Consider what you are comfortable with, how much you are willing to compromise, what you need and how your business and relationship will be best served.

Anything will work if you agree on it. Don't worry about setting up a traditional arrangement; set up what makes you both happy and works for your business.

What If You Both Want To Be Boss?

Sounds like trouble to many, no doubt. But when couples work together, it is not an uncommon arrangement. And why not? You have more strength when you operate as a unit. If you are planning and growing every phase of the business together, you both know the final word. So why not be able to say it?

> *"We're a team! I couldn't function without my other half."* D.Z., Rochester, MN

A united front is a powerful tool with employees and customers. They learn quickly they cannot play you against each other. Having more than one person to approach is an added service or convenience for your business. You have more flexibility knowing the other can handle things while you are away.

Although the style of your business is a major factor in determining the structure you create, many couples discover they are more productive if they work as a cooperative.

While it may seem inefficient for two people to be working on the same thing, attending the same meetings, making decisions about the same issues, or calling jointly on prospects or suppliers, it may prove to be twice as effective. Individuals are attuned to different stimuli. The cliche, "two heads are better than one," expresses the potential for collecting information, gaining insights, relating to people, analyzing data, and generating new ideas.

Similarly, there are certain personalities that are attracted to each other. If one of you seems more compatible with certain customers, employees, or clients, and no credibility will be lost, why not capitalize on the situation and relinquish the spotlight to the most effective partner?

Another benefit of sharing equal posts is the comfort of knowing that someone can relieve or rescue you on those inevitable days or moments when you lack energy or ingenuity.

The danger in this parallel arrangement is being condescending, sarcastic or angry when you disagree with a decision made by your partner. If the incompatible decision cannot be neutralized, hurt feelings, hostility and emotional separation can become serious problems. Some ways to handle disagreements are covered in Chapter 8 on Conflict Resolution.

> *"Think before speaking in anger — once said, words can not be taken back."*
> *Maryallen Estes, Burnsville, N.C*

Two horses pulling a carriage works. The weight of the carriage is equally distributed. They turn together, halt together and run together. If it's a two-horse carriage, one horse could not do it for long without becoming exhausted and devastated.

On the other hand, there are some carriages that perform better with one horse in the lead. What kind of carriage do you have?

Some Businesses Require A "Boss"

In some cases, it is better for the company if one partner takes the lead or a least *appears* to be the boss. For example: a company selling tools with a large male clientele may be aided by having a male authority as the final word, while a child care center would be regarded more securely with a woman at the helm.

> *"Even if we are co-owners and both active in the business, someone has to be the boss. This works when I am willing to act as second in command."* A.N., Jamestown, ND

Whether or not this is fair treatment to the sexes, it is a fact that as a society we are still prone to associate genders with certain conditions. Unless you are driven to overcome this discrepancy in perception, you have the perfect set-up as a Couple at Work to solve the problem: let the person who will best serve your company and its goals be the boss.

Some Thoughts About Titles

Inevitably when you are in business you will be asked "what is your title?" Some ask out of curiosity, some as a means to distinguish your place in the hierarchy, some want to know how to address, list and/or approach you, while others may ask hoping to condescend or embarrass you.

While titles are often used for public purposes, they can be another useful way for defining your position to yourself or giving you confidence when you meet the world. The fun in being a Couple at Work is having any title you want. Of course, if you plan to use it as a marketing device, it should apply to what you actually do, but it's also an opportunity to be creative, even playful. Your title can be used as a catalyst for conversation or a tool to help you develop an image.

In our survey, one man listed his title as "President/Top Dog" while another said he was "Assistant to Wife." Needless to say, to be effectively executed, non-traditional titles will have to work with the personality of the user and the image desired for the business. Many couples in the survey used titles to support their joint commitment and collaboration in the business such as co-owner, partner, or co-manager.

Another angle is not to use titles at all. Having no title or each using the same title such a Vice President, gives you flexibility with customers when you need to discuss an issue with your partner before making a final decision. You can always say you will have to talk to the boss.

Keeping in mind the goals of your company, your personalities and your needs, try to have fun naming your rank. It's just a title.

Dub

I'd created a real problem by interfering with Janet's job. Basically I didn't believe in the person I loved and trusted. But then, all I had to go on was what I saw.

Once she realized I was not a mind-reader and described her strategy, I felt a lot better. Her plan made sense and for the first time, in a long time, I felt hopeful. The relief I felt from understanding what she was doing was so unexpected.

She made her case quite clearly — either get out of her territory or do it all. Something a boss once told me flashed through my mind: 'don't defend an indefensible position' 'Face up and move on' was my only choice if I wanted the company to flourish.

My decision and response came as fast as her statement. I could have been stubborn and refused to let go, but that would not have served me as a person, our company goals or our relationship.

Of course, my interference with the employees was already taking it's toll. They were getting the message; we could be played. We set about defining who was in control of what. It didn't take long to determine that even with our territorial authority, we each wanted and expected input from the other.

The company was small, usually with ten or fewer employees. Since the beginning, I had always held Monday morning staff meetings because I believed that employees had a right to understand the big picture and what was going on each week. It also served as an open forum for them to voice their own ideas.

At the next meeting I announced that, from now on, as far as they were concerned, Janet was the boss (they'd heard this before). Furthermore, I told them if I contradicted anything she said, they were to remind me of what I had just said. There was an undeniable hush. I suppose they were wondering if this was for real. It didn't take them long to catch on; the first time I did a backslide, they were quick to set me straight!

We became much more efficient after that. Things began to take shape. The sales staff had a training program, monthly goals, and weekly meetings; the warehouseman had performance plans and a course of action to organize the warehouse, and the office manager was no longer concerned that Janet was planning a job takeover. The operation began to purr like a fine-tuned machine. It started to be fun.

Janet

Of course I 'screamed' (his word) my frustration at his over-riding my orders and humiliating me to the warehousemen. He 'rationally' (his word) pointed out to me that our priorities were not to make a larger mess, but to get customers in and sales made. My response was something about his being blind, thoughtless and inconsiderate and how could I have ever got myself into such a mess.

The period that followed was miserable. I was afraid to say anything to anybody, I was afraid not to say anything to anybody. Dub and I were not feeling very...friendly. I felt small, incompetent and useless. I called a meeting.

One of the things I love about this man is that he listens. Instead of assuming that he saw things the way I did, I explained what I had in mind. I described my plan to slowly reorganize and to deliver to each employee a detailed plan of what was expected. Drawing from my past experience, I showed him that it was not an overnight success story, but that the method worked.

Furthermore, I asked him to understand how difficult it was for me to gain respect from the employees when it was obvious I had no authority although I was supposedly an equal partner.

Not only did he hear me, he acted upon it. The next day he called a staff meeting and with that 'I've been a naughty boy' grin of his, explained that now he was on the road so much, I was in charge. And if (he meant when) he came back and made comments that sounded contrary to my decisions, they were to ignore him! Now how can you be too hard on a man that good?

More Reading About Partners In Business

Barnett, Frank and Sharan Barnett, *Working Together,* Ten Speed Press, 1988.

Brothers, Dr. Joyce (hosted by) and Frishkoff, Patricia, *Couples in Business Together,* (videorecording), Austin Family Business, Oregon State University, 1996.

Karofsky, Paul I., *If Men and Women Are Equal...,* Northeastern Univeristy's Center for Family Business, March 1996.

Nelton, Sharon, *In Love and in Business,* Wiley, 1986.

O'Shea-Roche, Annette and Malmberg, Sieglinde, *Partners at Home and at Work,* Self-Counsel Press, 1994.

Partow, Cameron and Donna, *How to Work With the One You Love,* Bethany House , 1995.

Survey responses *to the question "What are you feelings about the business you are in?"*

> "Depends on the day."
> L.D.B., South Dartmouth, MA
> "Enjoy it more than I've enjoyed any other job." S.W. B., South Dartmouth. MA

> "Love it. Wouldn't do anything else."
> B.E., Chatham, MA

> "Burned out."   A.V., Troy, MA

> "Good — it allows us flexibility but it is overwhelming and always on our minds and in our lives." Kathleen Hubert, Newport, NJ

Chapter 5
The Invisible Woman

Dub

Between Janet and I the company was coming around nicely. Although the sales staff was grumbling about meeting goals and having to get out one day a week to drum up business, sales were increasing. We could see positive changes in the warehouse staff; they were taking pride in their work and were working hard to meet their weekly performance guidelines. I was settling into my new position and making larger and better buys.

One major glitch remained, however. The one thing I did not want was to come back to the shop after being on the road all day or week to face customers who refused to work with Janet. I had enough to do and Janet now knew pricing, overhead, overall cost and current inventory much better than I did.

It was happening over and over — big clients and wholesalers refused to acknowledge her authority. It was ridiculous. We were working as a team; we made all our decisions together and had equal input. I had never been so conscious of the injustice that women face until it affected someone I knew so closely. She did

67

not deserve this.

Janet

In the weeks and months that followed, the business gradually began to change shape. Dub was making excellent buys bringing in quality furniture, the employees had their performance plans and were accountable for them, the warehouse was looking good, and I was beginning to feel a sense of contribution.

Except for a few 'slip-ups' Dub stayed out of my territory and I stayed out of his. We were both involved in every decision, however. Every morning before the employees arrived we walked through the warehouse and jointly decided on a plan of action for the day. Before bidding on a load of furniture, we discussed how well suited it was to our image and customers, if we wanted to spend the money it required, and how to create the space needed to accommodate it.

At night and on weekends we talked and planned incessantly about each phase and detail. On Monday mornings we held staff meetings to present our plans and hear employee feedback. We began to project a united front. By listening to each other and voicing our opinions, we were able to understand each other's position. Our goals began to evolve more deeply into a joint venture.

I was gaining credibility by being dedicated and having visible influence in problem solving and decision making. My word was as good as Dub's. Equal partners — hmm, I was getting used to this stuff.

And then one day a customer walked in and wanted to negotiate a deal. After working with a salesman for some time and not getting the price he wanted I was brought into the scene.

His request was ridiculous. I tactfully agreed with the sales-man, offered as many alternatives as possible but stood firm. Finally he looked at me with a condescending smile and said, 'Have Dub call me when he gets back.'

EXCUSE ME?

Unfortunately, he was not the odd duck.

Must Women Roar?

Being a woman in today's world is leaps and bounds better than it used to be — but, exceptions aside, it's not there yet. Unless we make a decision to devote our lives full-time to women's rights, we must learn to deal productively with the situations that regularly occur.

As a woman, rarely is attention directed at your partner because you are considered inept. It is an injustice of our society that we look to men as leaders and authority figures, regardless of how things really are.

> *"Often clients prefer to speak to Al and treat me like a clerk." A.F., Rome, GA*

When you are competent, creative and a fully contributing member of any team you want to be recognized as such. You are just as tired, frustrated, thrilled, challenged, and invested as your *equal* partner. You may even be the one who started the business, spends more time and energy in it or be the engine that makes it purr.

To deny your feelings is not a recommended choice. Being angry, disgusted, frustrated or even jealous at the injustice of being dismissed in deference to a male figure are natural reactions. It's unfair, ignorant and insulting behavior.

Fortunately, there are a number of choices that work quite well, although patience and a sense of humor may be required. Channeling feelings that arise from lopsided thinking into a flow that is comfortable and satisfying is the key. To be recognized and valued for their worth, women need to be self-confident, persistent and yes, willing to work hard to get it.

Lighten Up Ladies

In the book *What Mona Lisa Knew*, Dr. Barbara Mackoff sites a survey taken of 200 executives asking what kept women from succeeding. Their overwhelming response? Lacking a sense of humor!

No doubt about it; women have rightfully been concerned about not being taken seriously in the workplace. Clearly women who possess expertise, skills and the ability to achieve superior results have earned the right to be noticed and admired. But is there some confusion between serious and somber?

Is it possible to be serious and playful too? People gravitate toward happy, smiling faces. They feel more comfortable and less threatened. Jack McAllen, in his book *The Boss Should Be a Woman,* says that in many cases men are afraid of women. If so, a woman wearing a frowning, defensive expression will be even more formidable.

Learning to get back in touch with your lighter side has many benefits. It allows you to be less self-conscious and more your own special style. You will be more likely to defuse tense situations, less likely to blow up, cry or be overcome with emotion. Your softer approach will diminish anger and defensive reactions and help you develop better relationships.

So how does one go about being lighthearted in such a heavy-handed world?

◆ **Develop an attitude:** Dr. Mackoff says being a "good-humor woman is a state of mind." Become conscious of the benefits of being more fun-loving and try to attract them through your actions and reactions.

◆ **Seek out the laughable:** Read the funnies, rent comedies, go to comedy houses, and study people who are successful and enjoy life. Read funny books and stories. Collect cartoons. Feed your mind with humor until it understands.

◆ **Gain a new perspective:** When dealing with a stressful situation, imagine yourself in a movie. Sometimes stepping outside yourself changes the entire mood. Or try to picture how the scene would look if you were standing on the north rim of the Grand Canyon. Project five, ten or twenty years into the future and see yourself telling someone about the situation. Would it look as important?

◆ **Stop trying to be perfect:** Do a good job. Do a great job, but if things get goofy every now and then, so what? Plan for things to go wrong sometimes and prepare a humorous approach. Suppose you are giving a speech and asking for questions but no one responds. What will put everyone at ease? A blush and a mumble? Or a grin and a lighthearted remark such as "Silence is golden and now I'm rich."

> *"Men and women don't think alike."*
> Donna Marriott, St. Augustine, FL

◆ **Recognize the difference between male and female humor:** In their usual style, women tend to be more cautious and sensitive when joking around with their pals. They consider it complete taboo to make cracks about the weight problem or wrinkles of a girlfriend and feel concern if a fellow female were to trip or fall down.

Men on the other hand, readily kid each other in ways that women consider mean or inconsiderate, and then go out to lunch as though nothing happened. They laugh raucously if a male buddy tips over in his chair or experiences a clumsy encounter that women would consider humiliating. Men often express affection to their friends with an insulting comment. Somehow they seem to know it is all in play.

For women who become targets of men's humor, the best defense is to be prepared *not to be defensive!* Unless you want to spend a lot of time and energy trying to educate them as to how you feel and how you want them to kid you, learn to respond with a smile and a good-sport remark.

Of course, if a man is truly offensive or harassing you have no choice but to use other tactics. For well-intended humor, understanding that men have a different approach will support you in developing a new reaction.

> *"For nine and a half years the BOSS was me — now it is great to share that. If there is a question or problem the staff still defers to me. But it is funny to see strangers come into the office and expect the last word to come strictly from the MAN. Lots of times it is great to hide behind! We have a great give and take relationship. I'm proud of him!"*
> A.B., Raleigh, NC

Once you have decided to go about life with a lighter view, being ignored because you are a woman can actually be an opportunity for amusement. After all, who's the joke on when a customer demands to see your male counterpart who then comes to you for a decision?

Or what about the times you're in a meeting and the eye contact is riveted on your partner even though your input is equally important? By all means do your part and make your contributions, but don't waste energy fighting for the spotlight. Work the scene to your advantage.

When attention is diverted from you, pay attention to details that may be missed when the focus is on you. Concentrate on the other participants' words. Look for gaps or unclear statements. Consider if what they are saying is pertinent and accomplishes what you intended. You will be surprised how much this contributes to the overall comprehension of a meeting.

Being amused at life is not about telling jokes all day or spewing sharp, caustic one-liners. It is bigger than that. It embodies a lighter look at all of life with reactions that are alert, relaxed and gentle. It is not belittling yourself or others, but rather making fun of situations. A little effort towards developing a sense of humor makes life more pleasant but it also makes you, as a woman, more approachable and more likely to be recognized.

Capture Them With Confidence

Being timid, unsure or indecisive does not suit anyone, particularly women who have a purpose to be recognized as an equal and vital force in a business partnership. Learning to develop a presence that exudes sureness without being cocky or superior is a valuable tool in your quest to be taken seriously.

♦   ***Be informed:*** There is no better insurance for self confidence than knowing what you are doing. If you speak from knowledge (not stubbornness), you are more likely to be heard than if you are hesitant due to incomplete details.

◆ **Get involved in relationships:** Work closely with customers and employees often to build their assurance that you are capable and able to solve problems to their satisfaction.

◆ **Believe in yourself:** Women have qualities that are in demand in today's workplace. With companies and corporations demanding people with relationship building skills to improve customer service and leadership, women are naturals. Many men are having to learn the skills that women have practiced for years.

◆ **Use your history as your guide:** Focus on achievements you have accomplished on your own. Consider skills and qualities you used to realize these events. They are still within you whether you use them or not.

◆ **Don't forget your sense of humor:** As long as you are not belittling yourself, a sense of humor gives the impression that you are comfortable with yourself and therefore more approachable. When you react defensively or with anger, you may project a lack of self respect, an ingredient that alienates others from you.

Jack McAllen has a theory called "Self-Confidence: If It Is To Be — It Is UpTo Me." It is about making the decision to take control of yourself and where you are going with your life. It is about being confident in your abilities, strengths and achievements. "This attitude of greatness, of being in complete control of oneself, of strength to achieve and of knowing you will win is the basis of gaining all that is good and equal in this new era for women," says McAllen.

Talk To Be Noticed

Often enough to warrant attention is the fact that men and women seem to use the same words and somehow mean different things. Although they seem to have the same thoughts, and even the same goals in mind, they seem to quite regularly say things that are entirely misunderstood by one another.

Women can benefit by learning to interpret what men are saying and why they say it. Of course men can benefit from doing the same about women, but this is about women developing skills to be recognized and appreciated in a "man's world."

> *"Even though I've been in sales longer and have a good business sense, sometimes my ideas are rejected out of hand because of my presentation to my partner. He feels I am condescending at times and will not listen to me."*
> Jean Panko Kaplan, Gurney, IL

Deborah Tannen, author of *You Just Don't Understand,* explains why there is such a disparity in the way men and women use conversation.

Men, she says, are engaged in a world of one-upmanship. To them, conversations are negotiations to see who will come out on top. Although they desire intimacy and involvement, their core driver is enjoying life as a contest in which they try to remain independent and protect themselves from the attempts of others to put them down.

Women on the other hand, she says, use conversation to build relationships. In their world, the focus is on connection and community. Their concern about status and failure takes a back seat to the primary goal of uniting people.

She emphasizes the importance of accepting these differences as just that — differences, not right or wrong, just different.

With two such different perspectives of what life is all about, it is easy to see why men and women so often misunderstand each other. Suppose you are in a meeting of mixed gender. Men tend to make statements and proceed to back them up with lots of evidence and reasons to support their statements.

Women may make statements on subjects they are thoroughly educated about and then ask for input, trying to build consensus, and reach a team conclusion. In a man's world, asking for the opinions of others about a statement is perceived as weak and insecure, qualities that may leave many women unjustly in the dust of mediocrity.

The assumption that a woman is less of a decision maker or authority figure than a man is made as many times by women as by men. So, if blame is to be applied it will have to be to the transitional stage that we occupy as a society. As a populace, our attitudes have not reached the state of seeing complete gender equality in the workplace.

Projecting outward hostility, arguing for your rightful position or demanding loudly to be acknowledged will probably not win you the kind of recognition you prefer. Instead, you will probably fuel the idea that as a woman, you react emotionally and do not know how to handle a business transaction competently.

In the workplace where women are fighting to be acknowledged, it pays to study the ways men relate and, if it serves your purpose, adapt. It is not about playing games. It is using all the tools at your disposal to contribute and be acknowledged for doing so.

Remember, you are bringing moves to the table that men are

having to learn to survive in today's world. It's about sharing what works.

Of course, for Couples at Work, it never hurts to have your partner on your side.

Men Can Help

Many males of Couples at Work are just as frustrated by the lack of regard for their partners as viable authority figures as the women themselves. Often in a business environment, men develop a new level of respect and appreciation for their partners' abilities.

> *"The last three years of working with my wife have blown a lot of the macho, 1950's stereotypes I grew up with."*
> *A., Annapolis, MD*

In many cases, men rely on their partners for information, planning and problem solving. If they are called upon to settle a dispute, they may have to refer to their partner for facts or details before making a decision.

A man may also feel annoyed by a misinterpretation of power if an issue falls outside his designated area of responsibility. He may not have the necessary data or technical expertise to handle every circumstance. Or he may have his hands full taking care of his own duties. To disperse his energies for the sake of being perceived as "the one in charge" is not always in his best interest.

> *"Learn to control your ego. Try to put yourself in her shoes every now and then. Remember, she has to work with you also. J.P.L., Dothan, AL*

Men, there are ways you can help support your partner in

developing an image of equality and eliminate the idea that you are the ultimate authority.

- ◆ ***Acknowledge her authority in public:*** If a customer defers to you when it is your partner's area of responsibility, you can accommodate the customer, but tactfully explain that she will be the contact in the future.

- ◆ ***Announce her position:*** If it is appropriate for your business, send out notices to clients, call them on the phone or if they come in, introduce her as your partner. Your words presenting her as an equally solid source for service, information and support as a decision maker sends a subtle but strong message.

- ◆ ***Assure her training:*** If your business is already established when she joins you, it can be awkward enough without knowing what she is doing. The benefits of providing sound training where needed will be enjoyed by both partners.

- ◆ ***Give credit where credit is due***: When she comes up with an idea that is significant or visible, tell everyone that it was her ingenuity that bore it.

- ◆ ***Back her up:*** When a decision she has made is presented to you for re-negotiation, stand firm that her decision is final.

If you don't agree with what she has offered and are concerned that your business will be hurt if concessions are not made, discuss it in private and let her be the one to approach the client with a new offer.

> *"It was painful to rid myself of my genetic chauvinism."* J.P.L., Dothan, AL

To leave your egos at the door (or assume your wego at the door) and be in this together goes a long way toward maneuvering the situation.

A man who publicly and sincerely maintains his partners' position as equal to his own, will amass his fortune in loyalty and support from her. With these elements and others echoing between them, Couples at Work are equipped to accomplish great things.

Women Are Gaining Ground — Slowly But Surely

Although there are many things women can do on a day to day basis to claim their rightful position, it may also help to be aware that the movement toward equality is underway.

Persistence and patience pay big rewards. By handling yourself professionally, making effective decisions and contributing in a full and positive way, you are taking steps toward being taken seriously. Mix in a sense of humor and a pleasant, assertive manner, and you will eventually be given the respect you deserve.

On a broader scale, be aware that forces are slowly paving the way for women to take their fitting place in the world of business. "Women are now starting businesses at nearly twice the rate that men do. Women will be starting up more than half of all businesses as they claim their position in the economy," says Thomas Bettridge in an article written by Tracey Rosenthal Drury for the July 1995 issue of *"Business First of Buffalo."*

Women have reached "a critical mass in virtually all the white-collar professions, especially in business," according to statistics collected by John Naisbitt and Patricia Aburdene for reproduction in *Megatrends 2000*. Since 1972, the percentage of women physicians has doubled, women have achieved "if not a majority, a substantial porportion of the previously male-dominated careers in the information and service industries."

Additionally, they say that in finance "women have reached the halfway point" meaning that more than half of all officers, managers and professionals in the nation's fifty largest commercial banks are women.

Faith Popcorn in *The Popcorn Report,* sites a new spring of enlightened groups such a WISE-UP (Women's Issues Swing Elections-Unite Politically) and WISH LIST (Women In The Senate and House). These groups, she says, are "not to put down men, but to shift the balance."

There are hundreds of examples representing the progress of women in our society. It is happening, although not fast enough and complete enough to make the differences magically manifest themselves in our everyday lives. The shifting is tedious and painstaking, but the gears are turning.

Dub

Part of the reason clients were resistant to doing business with Janet was that she was new and had not yet established a rapport with them. They wanted to work with a familiar face. I had run into the same problem with my former partner when I was in her position. Even though I actually owned the business and had the last word, he had a long history of contacts. I understood her frustration on this account.

But the main reason was probably that she was a woman in a male-oriented business. She was interfering with the good-old-boy-network and they tried to avoid her like the plague. It wasn't in my best interest to encourage them. She was a better negotiator and salesman. I gave things away and she didn't, which was one of the reasons we started making more money.

It could have been tougher, but I had plenty of motivation to back her up. I had my hands full trying to keep up with my own responsibilities. We were more profitable and I sure as hell wanted to keep her happy.

Gradually they began to get the message that she was the end of the line and funny thing — I don't think we ever lost any business over it!

Janet

It took time to establish myself with the regulars. If Dub hadn't stood behind me, I might have folded. In all my experience I had never worked in a strictly man's world. Any gender discrimination I'd been confronted with in the past had just rolled right past me. This was different. It was blatant and alarming.

Dub had such a great way of handling things. He took a lot of flack about letting a woman 'take control.' But he had a way of grinning and shrugging that most people couldn't resist anymore than I could. They knew just by looking around that he was doing the right thing; the product he was bringing in was certainly to their advantage, the service was better and people were friendly and helpful.

After awhile, people became really fascinated with our operation. They had witnessed the changes in mood and physical qualities. Many of them wanted to know in detail how we did it. And eventually, many of them actually asked me!

More Things To Read About Women

Drury, Tracey Rosenthal, *Women Take Greater Roles in Growth of Small Business,* Business First of Buffalo, July 1995.

Frishkoff, Patricia A. and Brown, Bonnie M., *Women on the Move in Family Business,* Business Horizons, March-April 1993.

Gorman, Christine, *How Gender May Bend Your Thinking,* Time, July 1995.

Gumpert, David E., *New Directions New Opportunities,* Working Woman, October, 1995.

McAllen, Jack, *The Boss Should Be A Woman,* Blue Dolphin Press, 1993.

Mackoff, Barbara, *What Mona Lisa Knew,* Lowell House, 1990.

Shannon, Jacqueline, *Why It's Great to be a Girl,* Warner Books, 1994.

Ross, Ph.D.Ruth, *Prospering Woman,* Bantam Books, 1985. Sprankle, Judith K., *Working it Out, the Domestic Double Standard,* Walker,1986.

Tannen, Deborah, *Talking From 9 to 5,* W. Morrow, 1994.

Survey responses *to the question "Why did you select the type of business you have?"*

> "I wanted no landlord and no employees.
> A small Bed and Breakfast
> seemed to fill that need."
> P.B., Healdsburg, CA

> "It definitely suits our personalities, talents
> and interests. We wanted to work together
> and we like being home."
> A.L., Austin, TX

> "We were competing against each other in
> our last business, so we changed to
> something neither of us knew. He has his
> jobs and I have mine."
> J.C., Key West , FL

Chapter 6
Money Matters

Dub

I grew up believing money was your life blood. If you didn't have money you weren't a man, you were a nobody. Although my life experiences taught me differently, I still couldn't shake the feeling. In my 30's and 40's this concept reached a fever pitch. What money I could raise, I bet life and limb on the big score. I never quite measured up to my expectations.

I started the company literally without a dime, but much to my surprise found I had a good head for business. Money was tight but I was never in the red.

My original partner was a good teacher when it came to bidding jobs even when we didn't have enough money. We would pre-sell half the product to other wholesalers or large retail clients thereby making enough money to pay for the load and freight before the bid money was due. The other half was brought into our warehouse at no cost.

Because I had very few living expenses, at the end of every month I took home only enough money to survive. I didn't have time for anything but the business so I didn't need any enter-tainment money. Clothes weren't an issue and I usually gulped down some fast food or didn't bother to eat at all.

After rent, salaries and bills, the rest of our income went toward buying product. I assumed when Janet came on board this routine would continue.

I think I should have told her that.

Janet

Money is a funny thing in my life. There were times when I had more money than I needed. But a single mother for many years and later a free spirit entrepreneur who gave up a secure and promising future in the 'Great American Corporation,' there were many more times when I could barely make ends meet.

No matter which way it was going, I somehow found ways to do things - take trips, frequent restaurants and invest in things that were meaningful to me. I really didn't worry much about money and things always had a way of working out. My curious and thirsty-for-experience nature would have it no other way.

In business I was much more reluctant to spend money on non-guaranteed returns. I preferred to analyze an expenditure to death (often literally) before dumping any of my precious funds on it!

By the time I went to work with Dub, I was in one of those comfortable phases, although I still had some major debts leftover from my less-than-comfortable phases. We discussed the money thing up front the same way we'd discussed our responsibilities; I assumed I'd get what I'd given up and he assumed I'd get what he decided — and that meant skipping breakfast, lunch and dinner.

What? Was he crazy?

Same Money — Different View

Differences in money management occur in all types of relationships. Opposing perceptions about the purpose of money and how it should be spent is a hot issue between partners. It is not uncommon to see a spendthrift paired with a miser, a risk-taker with the security-conscious, a hoarder with a squanderer, or an avoider with a confronter.

Most disagreements stem from differing *priorities* as to how money should be spent. "Couples who fight about money argue more often about how it is to be spent than about how much they have," say Blumstein and Schwartz in *American Couples*.

Men and women, whether or not they are working together, are motivated to approach money management by different forces.

> *"Unscientifically speaking, men and women are different."* G.L., Rome, GA

Some money habits seem to be gender intense. Men often view money as the path to power, position and acceptability to the world, and specifically to the women they love. Women are typically concerned with the security and social prestige that money offers. There are many books that explore the subject of how men and women developed these seemingly gender-specific beliefs.

For the purpose of this book, the important thing is to understand and acknowledge that different viewpoints are brought to the table by men and women and then get them to work for you.

Women Need Men

Although later in life this often subsides, men are typically driven by the big picture. They rarely envision their ultimate goal as a little shop in the neighborhood bringing enough income to pay the monthly bills and take a few vacations.

Instead, they see the local shop as a meager stepping stone to the national chain of well known and lucrative establishments. They think in terms of "how many millions can I make?" And "how fast can I make them?" Their thoughts are literally about fame and fortune.

This vision requires a lot of time and energy. If they think "play," it is probably along the line of golf so they can network for business, or "toys" so they can elevate their status in the eyes of their competition.

Men are willing to take big financial risks because they understand that in order to make money they have to spend money. If it requires risk, which it almost always does, well, that's just part of it. Men do not have to learn this, they just know it.

Eavesdrop sometime on a group of men talking business. Listen to the tales of success they weave without missing a beat. Quite possibly, they will be discussing how they are taking their business international; how they are going to merge with a multi-million dollar company; or how they are going to service the largest maker of widgets for the rest of their life. Not "how?" but "how!" They are like buckets with no bottoms. The ideas spew forth like fireworks on the 4th of July except they never fall to the ground. Instead, they are lifted to unbelievable heights, with no obstacles, no downturns, and no chance of burnout.

If you were to sit in on one of these sessions you would experience a lesson in unlimited thinking, creativity and visualization. And that's why women need men.

Men Need Women

Women in business, are driven by quite a different force. They want satisfaction. They want balance. They want enough money to be independent and free to do things that bring pleasure into their lives. As a general rule, they do not want to work day and night to make millions of dollars and attain international recognition.

In their dreams, women have fulfilling careers, go home, spend time with their families, make love, have friends, develop other interests, and play. They may play golf to network, but they mostly play because they like it. They think about success but in a much more controlled sense. They are happy with the local shop and envision being known in the community as having the best product, best service and cultivating satisfied customers.

Women, too, understand the principle of spending money to make money. But they are willing to do so in a much more calculated sense, risking less and enjoying a slow but steady return while enjoying other aspects of life simultaneously.

For contrast, listen to what women are saying when they get together to talk business. They are talking about better ways to market, how to improve their sales skills and better techniques to manage and develop their employees. They are making a quilt. One square at a time and they haven't skipped any stitches. They know how it will look when they are finished; each square completed and beautiful; all part of a solid, but modest whole.

Success in business is feeling proud and fulfilled. It is making enough money to be free, and that means being well rounded, being "all that you can be." And that's why men need women.

Different Money Styles Can Dance

Probably the single most significant factor in dealing with opposition is understanding. As a Couple at Work, if you agree to an open-minded discussion of perceptions about money management, you have begun to move towards mingling your differences.

> *"We have learned to discuss and look at the whole picture and each angle."*
> *Kathy Larson, Sandy, UT*

The first step in this process is to believe as a Couple at Work with different viewpoints, you have a unique tool with which to grow your business and your relationship. By meshing and balancing your opposing attitudes, you are opening the door to financial and emotional riches.

If you believe in the idea that when you strive for the moon you will at least meet up with a star, you are well on your way to understanding why the male vision is so important. As a woman, adopting even a fragment of the male perspective can move you to experience yourself, your partner and your life in ways you never imagined.

Flexible, open-minded thinking coupled with a cooperative experimentation of his money style is an opportunity to realize a greater sense of self, have more materially and be closer to your partner.

Men, on the other hand, have a lot to gain by sampling the perseverance women display in trying to achieve balance in their lives. By learning to pace your achievements and nourish yourself, your spouse and children along the way, you may avoid disappointment, fractured relationships and the emptiness that often accompanies one-track vision. By embracing a slice of the female direction, you may actually have a better chance of realizing all your goals.

As a Couple at Work, you are once again in a position to create that magic third entity. By resisting the temptation to plod along in old habits and courageously testing and mingling the paths of your partners, you have put in motion an explosive tool for success.

Resolving Your Money Differences

Being in love *and* in business gives you a hearty catalyst for resolving your money differences. In order to run a successful business and relationship, you will need to strive for common ground on how you actually disperse the precious revenue you collect.

> "We talk about the problems and don't try to overpower one another. We look at all the pluses and minuses."
> D.A., Troy, MA

A good place to start is with your individual aspirations for your business. Determining why you are in it, what type of growth you expect, your ultimate purpose for being in business and what kind of lifestyle you hope to achieve will help you determine if you are on the same track or if there are areas that need compromise or alteration.

Create a round table for two and discuss the following as they relate to your attitudes about money.

♦   *Purpose:* Do you see your business as a vehicle for producing unlimited income? Is your business mainly a source of independence to provide just enough money to cover your immediate lifestyle needs? Is it a source of retirement income? Is it a stepping stone to another venture?

Do you plan to sell it and do something else? Are you doing something you feel so passionate about that money is not a primary issue? Is your business primarily a basis for pride and recognition?

Are you fulfilling an obligation to a family business or member? Is your primary purpose to leave a legacy to be passed on through generations?

◆   ***Growth:*** What kind of growth do you hope for your business? One store, one location? Internal growth only, i.e. revenue increase without increased physical expansion or the addition of employees?

Two locations, many locations? National presence? Global? When will the growth occur? What factors will signify the time for expansion — financial goals or security, economic movement, customer demand, or recognition?

◆   ***Clientele:*** Do you plan to attract the masses or are your customers part of a niche? Are they upscale, middle class, lower income? Are they local, national or worldwide? How will you reach them and what will you spend? Will they come to you or will you go to them?

◆   ***Compensation:*** Will you take draws? How often? Will they be equal? How much will they be? What will determine the amount and frequency of draws?

Will you take only enough to cover your necessary personal expenses or will you take draws whenever you need them? Will your draws be determined by what is left over at the end of the month? If you don't take draws what will you use to live on and for how long?

◆ **Pension:** Is having a traditional pension plan important to you? Do you think putting money aside regularly for this purpose is necessary?

Would you rather bank on the value of your business to cover your retirement? How do you feel about providing retirement plans for employees? Do you plan to rely on the advice of a professional financial planner?

◆ **Philosophy:** How do you want your company to be seen by others? Will you be known as having the best service, the fastest service, the highest quality of product or service?

Do you plan to be the frontrunner in technology, always using the latest equipment and providing the most current information and availability? Is your ideal to move product in and out quickly, always having new inventory or techniques to offer?

Do you want to be the first one thought of when quantity or details are required? Do you want to provide an upbeat cheery environment or would you rather have a leisurely atmosphere where customers feel comfortable browsing or talking for hours?

Will you be known for your efficient delivery and follow-up, getting the most for the money?

◆ **Product/Service:** Will your product or service be the top-of-the-line in quality, accuracy and pricing? Or will it have mass appeal, a more common, affordable allure? Will it be considered expensive and worth it, economical, a good buy for the money, or a throw-away-and-replace kind of good?

Is competition a consideration or will your product or service be so unique that it stands alone? Will it be priced competitively, to move quickly, attract only certain customers?

◆ ***Long and short term financial goals:*** Do you plan to make enough to expand? In what time period? Do you want enough to live what you consider a comfortable lifestyle, pay the mortgage, maintain the business, take a few vacations, play golf, put the children through college, build a retirement nest?

Do you want enough money to be a giant in the industry? Do you plan to earn enough to make the business marketable and sell it? Do you hope to have enough money to support employees, family members, friends?

◆ ***Profits:*** Will they be re-invested back into the business? In part or in whole? Will they be divided between the two of you or will you gift them to family members or charity? Do you think management of profits should be handled only on the advice of a professional consultant?

◆ ***Budget:*** Do you plan to have separate accounts for your business and your personal finances? Will your business records be carefully tracked and categorized — regularly or at tax time? Is it important to set up separate accounts for tax reserves, sales, city, county, and federal? Will you make your quarterly tax payments on time?

Do you plan to draw up a formal budget to plan for advertising, promotions, inventory, salary increases, professional consultation, etc.? Will you offer credit; how will it affect cash flow and how will you collect?

Couples handle things differently. There are no right or wrong answers. For example, some Couples at Work recommend that regular salaries are the only way a person will feel worthy and appreciated. In our survey, 30% take draws whenever needed and 30% take a standard salary on a regular schedule. Others feel strongly about reaching their monetary and growth goals quickly, take only what is necessary and reinvest every extra cent back into the business.

> *"Respect each other's opinions and ideas.*
> *Compromise on differing issues."*
> *Anonymous*

Johansen and Brown in *A Guide to Marriage & Money* say that the ideal approach to money "is to view it as a tool — a tool which you are using to achieve what you want to achieve together in your life." Finding common ground and what works in your particular relationship is the key. Respecting each others' needs and attitudes and having a mutual understanding of what you want from your business will give you a reference point from which to make financial decisions.

What If You Just Can't Dance?

Sometimes, even though you discuss everything and are clear about your aspirations, you still can't come to agreements as to how the finances of the business should be handled. Chances are you have the same problem with your personal budget.

Additional tactics in resolving your money conflicts are needed as the problems are deeper than merely having a joint understanding of what you want from the business. Cheer up. You are far from alone and there is help available.

In her book, *Money Harmony*, Olivia Mellan discusses the

common attitudes of men and women regarding money. She talks about the basic cultural differences that we have carried through the ages when men were hunters and gatherers vying against one another for prey while women were caretakers, preparing and distributing the nourishment. These differences translate, then and now, into competition and risk for men while women tend to hoard — or build security — and distribute the goods as needed or as they see fit.

She claims, as do many other experts who study the differences of men and women, that although our society has changed dramatically from the primitive demands of ages ago, the genes and therefore the behaviors of the old life form still exist to some degree in present day.

Obviously, we have evolved to meet many of the requirements of our current society, but the seemingly ongoing struggles we experience in our relationships ask us to search for explanations. Although certain traits seem to be more common to each gender, it would be unfair to flatly label men as being one way and women being another. For the purposes of resolving money differences, there is no need to be gender specific. As a Couple at Work, you have your livelihood as well as your relationship at stake. Finding solutions are vital.

> *"To make living and working together easier, take the long view!"* L.M., Alton, IL

The goal is to assess your individual money styles, share them with each other and take steps necessary to come to understanding and agreement.

♦ **Desire:** The first ingredient for conflict resolution of any sort is desire. You must want to reach an equitable and agreeable solution and you cannot come to the table with the intent of changing your partner. If you cannot do this, then go no further until you can.

Keep in mind that we are often attracted to people who have opposite styles and then later, these styles irritate us. If we went beyond our irritation, we might admit that our partner displays qualities that we would like to have, at least to some degree.

◆ *Past:* Explore your early associations with money and how you arrived at them. What was it like growing up? Was money plentiful or scarce? Was it secretive or public? Did your parents feel ashamed of their lack of money or quiet about their abundance? How was money spent? What kinds of things were purchased?

Were you ever given money or did you always have to earn it? Were you encouraged to share your "wealth" no matter how large or small? Did you feel guilty if you spent money on yourself or for anything that wasn't considered essential?

Did money have spiritual or religious connections such as being evil or deserved prosperity? What did it represent — status, power, fun, or necessity? Did money equate to work?

◆ *Present:* How many of your associations from the past are alive and well in your present? Do they apply to your current life?

◆ *Interpretation:* Ask yourself what having money means to you. What do you expect from the accumulation of money? Do you expect control, recognition, or position? Do you believe that without it you will be more righteous, more sacrificial, and thereby a better person?

Do you think if you had more money you would be happy? Have you ever had enough money and were you happy? Powerful? Does money mean security? Do you think if you have enough money you will never have to worry about anything?

Is money freedom? Do you want just enough money to support the lifestyle that you desire, to help family, friends, community, or prepare for your retirement? What do you expect to achieve with money — peace, recognition, validation as a person, and status?

Are your interpretations valid? Why?

In the television series, *Money and Marriage,* Dr. Wendy LeDoux counsels several couples who are experiencing money difficulties. Although money appears to be the problem, it is only a symptom of underlying perceptions about money.

For example, one couple is severely distressed because they have lost a lot of money resulting from a decision made by the husband upon the advice of an investment banker. His wife, who was not consulted about the investment, is angry, threatening to leave the relationship and focuses her energy on blaming him for having made such a bad decision. He responds by degrading her and calling her names.

What evolves as they discuss the situation are his feelings of being alone in the burden of their financial well-being. He feels inadequate and humiliated at having lost the money and is at his wits end thinking about the possibility of losing his family.

She, on the other hand, feels unimportant in the relationship, certainly less than an equal in decisions involving money, and is hurt and sad that he is calling her names. Her instinctive reaction is to get far away from him. Instead of supporting and reassuring him of her love, no matter what, she resorts to accusing him of stupidity and makes the problem worse by threatening to leave him.

By expressing their true feelings instead of reacting in hurtful destructive ways, they are able to reach for the first time a real understanding of each other's perspectives. She understands that he feels overwhelmed trying to meet their financial needs and he understands that he is not alone in the financial arena.

> *Working together is not always easy, but it is very satisfying as you have a mutual goal that you can aim for together." Anonymous*

By putting the emphasis on joint responsibility and decision making, they can move ahead as a team to meet their mutual goals. "Partners who feel they have equal control over how money is spent have a more tranquil relationship," say Blumstein and Schwartz.

There are many sources available to guide you through money problems. If you are unable to reach solutions by yourself, don't hesitate to enlist the help of a professional either through books, consumer credit counseling services, videos, or money counselors. It's important! Do it!

Dub

I worried constantly about the overhead and how to keep the company afloat. But I also liked living on the edge. I knew if it came to it, I could sell a section of the warehouse product, but the game was to win bids and pay for product with other people's money and still bring in loads of furniture. It was like a big monopoly game.

I was doing my usual routine one day, going from office to office viewing furniture, when I ran into the load of a lifetime.

There was so much quality product, I could just see the huge sales figures. I knew we didn't have the money to pay for it if I won the bid, but it was so much and it was so nice! It would be a risk but the payoff would be well worth it.

Risk was my friend. It was the adrenaline that gave my life excitement and energy. It was risk that had started the company and later allowed it to add 20,000 square feet to the original 3600 in a short time, and another 10,000 after Janet arrived.

Janet and I were doing everything together now and when I went to her with the deal, she looked at me like I was crazy. She didn't understand about pre-selling and it was her responsibility to manage the revenue we took in and make sure the bills got paid.

Fortunately, she believed in me and was open-minded enough to listen to what I had to say. I explained the method of my madness and pointed out the number of clients to whom we could pre-sell product. She agreed to take the chance. It was a big risk, but the odds were good.

It may have looked like the risk was about money, but it was really about ourselves and our staff. It was having faith in our abilities, our desires, our creativity and our determination.

As time went on, my attitude about money began to change in my personal life. I had always been very conservative about spending, mostly because I didn't ever feel I had enough. I suppose Janet began to rub off on me. She didn't worry about money, she enjoyed life whether she was scraping by or not and somehow she always had enough. It felt good.

Janet

It didn't take long to figure out there simply wasn't enough money to take large draws. We were working with a struggling new business in a reorganization stage. *The monthly overhead was enough to drain most of the income we collected from sales. Whatever was left had to buy product and pay our personal expenses.*

The first reward for experimenting with each other's money style began one rainy day in September. Dub was confronted with an opportunity to buy a choice lot of furniture but the price was high. It meant spending every cent we had including our monthly lease money which was due in two weeks. I was pretty relaxed about money, but I wasn't stupid. Couldn't we split the deal and the expenses with someone else?

Dub was convinced we could make it work. He showed me how we could pre-sell at least half the load before we even bought it and that by contacting our regular clients with photographs of the product, we could be sitting pretty in no time. I wasn't sure; it was a lot of stuff to sell in two weeks. And what about my bills? Wouldn't it be a lot safer to pass up this deal and buy a few smaller ones over a longer period of time. But...he had done it before.

I swallowed my fear and went for it. Not only did we make our rent back in time, but we had enough profit to buy more product and I made a hefty dent in my debt.

The big surprise was Dub suggesting we take a little vacation — just a weekend, but for a man who thought business and life were synonymous, it was like the dawning of a new age! We took the weekend trip, inhaled the fine aromas of the Napa Valley, and came back Monday fired up to hit it again!

It was time to hire another salesman.

More Reading About Money

Hoffman, Ivan, *The Tao of Money,* Prima Publishing, 1994.

Johansen, Frances, *Guide to Marriage and Money,* United Resources Press, 1991.

LeDoux, Wendy (hosted by), *Money and Marriage,* (videorecording), 1994.

Mellan, Olivia, *Money Harmony,* Walker, 1994.

Phillip, Michael, *The Seven Laws of Money,* Word Wheel, 1974.

Ward, John L. and Aronoff, Craig E., *Paying the Family: Common Problems,* Nation's Business, March 1993.

Survey response *to the question "Which method of compensation BEST describes your situation?"*

> "It's too new to take a salary."
> R.S., Lee's Summit, MO

> "When I am short on payroll, I have
> to hold my check."
> S.S., Lee's Summit, MO

> "Pay all the bills — enjoy it if any is leftover."
> Vickie Ragle, Mabank, TX

> "We never made money. It was all re-invested
> in the properties and equipment. We lived
> off our salaries and retirement."
> E.N., Austin, TX

> "The business is our home and the focus
> of who we have become."
> Steven Robbins, Benicia, CA

Chapter 7
Making Management Music

Dub

Although the roommate I'd brought on board and later had to fire was a short term solution to a long term problem, he was making sales. Janet was driving me nuts with her ongoing stream of interviews. I didn't think the salesperson she had in mind could actually exist. I kept reminding her, 'this is used office furniture we're dealing with here.'

In the 18 months before Janet, I had gone through six, seven, maybe eight salespeople and wasted a lot of time in instruction and training, but at least I had a warm body in there selling furniture. And yes, I know my management style wasn't everything it should be but the way things were going I had to establish priorities and my basic philosophy was any decision was better than no decision.

I just wanted her to get on with it.

Janet

Five weeks had passed since the problem salesman had been

fired. I'd been interviewing applicants at the rate of three or more a day but the one I was looking for hadn't arrived yet.

The one I wanted had to be part of our newly emerging image and that included being flexible, visionary, experienced, entrepreneurial, and loyal. Employees are investments, in my mind, and I'm willing to wait to get the right one.

Building a quality staff requires painstaking effort and the interviewing process had become a game too many knew how to play. Reading between the lines and listening to my gut feeling had become as important as asking the right questions.

I needed someone with whom I had rapport; I needed this person on my team and to be trustworthy with expert sales skills. I needed someone I could turn loose and not worry about how things were being handled. It was a big order and in the used furniture industry, attracting this type of person is a rare and valuable find.

Our one salesman kept sales steady but it was too much to ask for him to move product out at the same rhythm we were buying it. It wasn't the kind of position that could be handled with temporary help and although I pitched in when I could, there were too many other demands on my time to act as a full-time sales person.

The pressure was mounting and Dub was impatient. He wanted me to hire someone, anyone and do it yesterday! His style was to get a body and worry about it later. I thought about the last salesman...had he learned nothing?

Clearly, he wasn't the one who was going to have to deal with the situation when it went bad. He was getting on my nerves.

People Manage Differently

For couples that work together, having different management styles is almost a given. In our survey couples listed it as the second major problem in their working relationship. Many of these same couples say they can't imagine working with anyone else! How can that be? Most of them admit that they didn't start out so amiably. What did they learn? It seems what they learned was how to turn their differences into assets. How does that happen?

Personality Affects Management Styles

Although management style was ranked as the number two problem encountered by couples in their working relationships, it was a shift from what they were *worried* might be a problem *before* they began to be Couples at Work. While considering the move to build a business together, couples were most concerned about personality conflicts.

> *"Each of our strengths is the result of different personalities. It's the right brain versus the left brain and type A versus type B syndrome."* Alma M. Swiers, Calistoga, CA

Personality and management style are two distinct concepts, but it makes sense that personality has a lot to do with management style. Before you can effectively combine your opposing styles, it helps to understand your individual personalities and how you react to situations.

The words below describe personality characteristics. By identifying your reactions and preferences, you can begin to see what ingredients affect your personal management style.

With the descriptions that follow, you may relate to many at some level. Rate yourself on a scale of 0-3 with 0 being equal to

"I don't relate at all" and 3 being equal to" I relate to very much."

◆   ***Independent:*** You enjoy being alone, prefer to figure things out rather than ask for help, like being in control, enjoy leadership, and place a high value on personal freedom.

◆   ***Dependent:*** You seldom act or make decisions on your own, prefer group consensus, and dislike activities that require you to go it alone.

◆   ***Self-disciplined:*** You have good concentration, are persistent, are able to focus on results when working on a project, analyze your mistakes in order to learn from them, and have a strong personal drive and need to achieve.

◆   ***Restless:*** You have difficulty focusing, like to keep moving, are impatient for results, have little tolerance for people who operate differently than you, and are often discontented.

◆   ***Creative:*** You see problems as challenges; have innovative ideas; are curious, adaptive, intuitive, receptive to new ideas; and experiment with new ways of doing things.

◆   ***Determined:*** You find ways to do things that "can't be done;" are unyielding in your pursuit of a goal once you have made up your mind; are willing to make sacrifices, to achieve long-term goals; think of yourself as ambitious, positive, committed, gutsy, and motivated.

◆   ***Risk-taker:*** You take chances, believe that those who take risks are more likely to get ahead, live life to the fullest, have a high need for adventure, will gamble on a good idea, and are willing to experience failure for the sake of enlarging your perspectives.

- **Security conscious:** You are apt to act cautiously both physically and financially and guard your emotions; you collect all the facts and figures before moving ahead; believe that saving for the future is a must; take risks only if the odds are highly in your favor; and feel that training is important.

- **Confident:** You feel like a winner, believe in yourself and your unlimited potential, accept challenges, have strong self-esteem, can accept compliments, and are self-assured.

- **Tentative:** You are often unsure of yourself, shy away from situations that may spotlight you, ask for others' opinions frequently, and rely on others to make decisions.

- **Communicator:** You are rarely misunderstood; remain open-minded of others' opinions; have a good sense of humor; keep your word; are comfortable around people who are more successful than you; are a good listener; remember names and faces; can keep a confidence; are flexible, friendly, thoughtful, and reasonable.

- **Reserved:** You prefer not to speak up; say only what you think is important; are not always understood; are shy, remote and often considered aloof.

- **Leader:** You like people. You bring out their best, are consistent in your dealings with them, keep them informed of their progress, can motivate and influence them, encourage them to live up to their potential, can assign work to them without hesitation, and are fair and honest.

109

♦ **Follower:** You are comfortable carrying out the decisions and instructions of others; are supportive and interested in pleasing those in control; do not initiate ideas unless they are in support of activities already being performed; are willing to rearrange your schedule to accommodate others, and are usually agreeable.

♦ **Manager:** You see the big picture; understand the need for details; are decisive; able to delegate; take charge in a group; pass opportunities to others; are patient, approachable, authoritative, and give clear directions.

♦ **Subordinate:** You are most comfortable as an assistant; like to implement and pursue projects that have been initiated by others; prefer to deal with daily responsibilities rather than long term results and feel fulfilled by completing tasks assigned to you.

♦ **Organized:** You divide big projects into small chunks; set priorities and act on them; set deadlines and plan strategies on a daily basis that propel you to your goal; set long term and short term goals; educate yourself on current trends, techniques, and skills; and keep your work space orderly and your filing up-to-date.

♦ **Active:** You thrive on activity; prefer to ask for information rather than gather it yourself; rely on others for facts on current trends; like distraction from details; are often surrounded with people; are motivated by visionary ideas; like lively discussions and debate; have trouble focusing on end results or big picture outcomes; enjoy chaos and crisis, and have a disorderly work space.

♦ **Planner:** You meet deadlines ahead of time; set aside time to work without interruption; work well under pressure; use preventive measures to eliminate potential problems; plan for the unexpected, plan your work; do your most difficult projects first; do not "over book" yourself, and limit your activities.

◆ **Spontaneous**: You like adventure; often react to the spirit of the moment; rarely make schedules or to-do lists; use stress as a catalyst for action; promote excitement from unconventional behavior, and are not a traditionalist.

◆ **Academic:** You are analytical, impersonal and logical in drawing conclusions; rely on data and facts to evaluate situations; and need plenty of information to form a judgement.

◆ **Feeler**: You are warm, patient, empathetic and appreciate the value of feelings in others; often use your own experiences as a reference point to react; are concerned about how you will be perceived by others; and are sometimes too emotional, excitable or sentimental.

Compare your ratings with each other. If you are like most Couples at Work, you have each assigned different ratings to many of the descriptors. One of you gave a three to "independent, desire, risk-taker and manager," while the other gave three to "reliant, methodical, security conscious, and reserved." You may also have given the same ratings to certain characteristics.

Keeping in mind the ratings you applied to various characteristics about yourself, consider how a broader description of personality might apply.

Carl Jung, the famous Swiss psychoanalyst, promoted the notion that there are four basic personality styles, each owned to some degree by every human being. He said that one style is predominant in each of us and that it can be observed as early as infancy. In an article written for *Supervision* by Daniel Tomal, these styles are summarized.

♦ ***Intuitor:*** "The intuitor is a conceptualizer and sees things from a predominant perspective of innovation, creativity, theory, and imagination.

He is idealistic, future-oriented and visionary. He often seems to be in a world of his own. He often approaches his work with originality, but may be scattered in his thoughts...he may be creative and can sometimes be reckless and pose safety risks on himself and his co-workers.

His office or work area is often modern, colorful and abstract."

♦ ***Feeler:*** "The feeler appreciates the values of feeling and human emotions. He is often described as being personable, empathetic, perceptive, warm, patient, and sensitive to the feelings of other workers.

He can, however, be too emotional, excitable or overly sentimental. He tends to view things relative to the past and is more concerned about the feelings of workers than getting the job done. He tends to waste time on the job worrying about personnel problems.

He has a tendency to go along with tried and proven solutions to problems. His office or work area is often homey with lots of family pictures and plants."

♦ ***Thinker:*** "The thinker is very analytical, objective, systematic, and methodical. He is careful to organize his thoughts in a structured fashion, but is often criticized for being unemotional, controlled or rigid...is conservative, a slow decision maker and is not a risk-taker.

His office or work area tends to be organized and neat."

♦   ***Doer:*** "The doer is hard-driving, results-oriented and seems to have an unending amount of energy. He communicates to the point and often refers to the bottom line.

He is technically skillful, decisive, assertive, and pragmatic. He may be viewed as status-seeking and impatient. He may act first and think later causing mistakes on the job. He tends to view things from the time frame of the present.

His office or work area tends to be more on the messier side."

Which description do you most relate to? By recognizing your personality traits you begin to understand why you manage the way you do. Management is just another way you express your personality.

> *"We look at everything differently. He is detailed oriented. I see big pictures. He's a pessimist, I am an optimist."* Kathy Larson, Sandy, UT

It is easy to see why there will be conflict if one of you is a doer and the other a thinker. The doer expects results yesterday and the thinker must analyze a situation, sometimes delaying action for an extended time.

Combining an intuitor and a feeler has obvious consequences; the intuitor is dreaming up ideas and acting spontaneously, often without thought as to how others will be affected while the feeler is primarily concerned with how others feel. Disagreement can be found in any combination of personality styles.

But what about those personality traits you have in common and yet, when it comes to managing, you seem to be at odds? Shouldn't you be in perfect harmony?

No wonder Couples at Work find this an area of concern. What else can go wrong?

He And She Differences

Another ingredient for separation? Although numerous studies have found that men and women who pursue entrepreneurial lifestyles show no differences in personality traits such as persistence, aggressiveness, independence, achievement motivation, goal orientation, leadership, and risk-taking, they do reveal some differences in the way they manage.

Typically, men in business are competitive and objective. They tend toward control and punishment and reward systems. Women are equipped with interactive, relationship driven skills. They prefer consensus style decision making techniques, and are comfortable persuading rather than ordering.

To assume that men are better managers, or that women are better managers wouldn't hold much weight. Up until recently, men have been credited as entrepreneurial models. They have developed and raised successful businesses on their own and, if their spouses were involved it was in the role of support, menial tasks or less visible ways. Men have been proving their ability to manage well for centuries.

A female entrepreneur of the past typically started a business out of necessity. She may have been divorced, widowed or a mother with small children. Often she had little or no business experience and usually owned a small service-related enterprise. Today's female entrepreneur reveals quite a different image.

According to an article in *Business Horizons,* (March-April, 1993), written by Holly E. Buttner, the characteristic female entrepreneur of the 1990's is "middle to upper-middle-class, married with children, 30 to 45 years of age at start-up. She is often the first-born, college-educated daughter of a self-employed father...has worked in a larger organization, gaining skills and knowledge her forebears lacked."

Ms. Buttner goes on to say that "despite the myth that women lack business savvy, female-owned businesses have a survival rate comparable to men's. Entrepreneurial success, as measured by gross sales and market share, is the same for both male and female entrepreneurs."

Couples At Work Have The Best Of Both Worlds

Couples who grasp the value of these collective concepts of personality, management and historical successes can begin immediately to build on them. In review:

◆ Couples at Work often bring different personality traits which translate into management styles to the store. They are not necessarily gender-related, but often cause a lot of stress between partners.

◆ Men and women do have certain management qualities that are normally defined by gender. These include competition and control from men and relationship-building skill and intuition from women.

◆ Men and women have proven that both management styles work because they have been successful without each other.

In Chapter 1, we talked about the birth of a "third brain" and Barnett's wego when couples unite in a business environment. Once again, Couples at Work have the opportunity to develop a new and separate entity by combining their individual management styles.

> "We are two very different people from different backgrounds in many ways, but we maximize on our differences and similarities."
> Joyce Bundergaard, Denver, CO

Agreeing to behaviors that are truly detrimental to your business and your relationship obviously doesn't work, but before accepting without pause that annoying behavior has negative effects, clear your mind and try taking a fresh approach.

If you have taken the time to rate and define the characteristics of your individual personalities, you should be aware of which qualities are dominant and which are reserved in your makeup. Put your lists side by side and note where you differ and where you are alike or similar.

Creating A Joint Style

To effectively create a joint style, you need a few tools to make your time and energy worthwhile. Bring with you the desire to create something better, an open mind, a willingness to release control, an awareness of your business needs and, most importantly, an appreciation of your partner.

Set the scene with a discussion using the following guidelines.

♦   *Recall and share successes:* All Couples at Work had lives apart in one way or another before their joint business venture. Many had other jobs or even businesses.

     Some ran households or involved themselves in community events. Maybe you feel your greatest achievements are your children or childhood accomplishments. Bring up anything that makes you smile with satisfaction. You can either do this in your head quickly or make a written list.

♦ ***Define qualities you used:*** What skills, insights and talents did you use in the situations you just listed? Was it your initiative, your creativity or your enthusiasm that drove the event? Were you the support vehicle that gave it a foundation?

Did you change peoples lives because you listened, were patient or insightful? Did you discover a detail that made a difference? Did you influence or direct others to a greater good? Use the list and try to think of all the attributes you used; focus on the ones that seemed more natural and that you enjoyed.

♦ ***Acknowledge the success of each other:*** Ask questions, contribute comments and suggest qualities that may have contributed to the success. It will help you fully appreciate and invest in the success, and will give your partner a feeling of safety and recognition.

Do the same exercise with situations you avoided, jobs you continually put on "the bottom of the pile," and responsibilities that made you feel dull or tired. What qualities were needed to handle these situations more productively?

Now that you are holding clearly in your mind that you both have the ability to be successful and that different approaches work well with different personalities, you are in a good frame of mind to move forward.

> "We are both strong willed and can disagree. We've worked this out about as well as we can. I think — at least that's today's opinion." Donna Jean Siewert, Loudon, TN

The next step is simply see who is best qualified to do the

jobs required. To get started, list the functions required to operate your business or use the suggestions in Chapter 3. Break it down into as many details as you like. Have your personality ratings on hand.

Look at each function and consider the following:

♦   *Qualities:* What qualities are needed to carry it out? Does it need organizational, management, active, creative, or subordinate resources? Note how each of you measure up to these qualities.

Be careful with your analysis of qualities. The same quality can have two sides. For example, creativity can be academic or artistic. If you both score "3" on creativity, which kind of creativity does the job require and what kind do you have?

Another example is two people scoring high on independent, but one relates to making decisions about money, while the other is thinking about doing projects without direction or input.

Evaluate carefully how much of a particular quality is needed. Although marketing and personnel both require patience, is it in different degrees? Who is best suited for each? Differences in patience can also be seen in people who can spend hours calculating detailed numbers but have no tolerance for long meetings.

♦   *Education or training:* Who has the know-how to perform the function? Is it something that can be learned quickly or is there time for extended training?

♦   *Time:* How much time is needed to devote to this aspect of your business? Does it require a major or minor chunk of time, is it supervised, can it be delegated? Who has the time?

- **♦** ***Desire:*** Who has the desire to do the job? Being proficient at something does not guarantee interest. A person who is a natural sales person may hate sales. Or people who are social and build rapport easily may detest networking.

- **♦** ***Necessity:*** Some jobs have to be done no matter what. Can they be squeezed into your schedule or should you enlist help from another source?

If you take the time to honestly evaluate yourselves and your business, you will begin to notice that your management style is expressed through the degree of your personality traits. In many areas, you may see that by accepting each other's way you begin to offset and/or enhance your overall position.

For example, suppose you are developing an advertising campaign and plan to do all the legwork yourself. One of you may be analytical and understand the principles of marketing, while the other is a feeler and knows how to reach people on an emotional level.

If the analytical partner handles the campaign, it will be strategically placed and timed. The message may be factual and to the point. It may work just fine. If the feeler partner is in charge of the campaign, the message will go right to the heart of the customer, be placed appropriately and it may also work just fine.

But if the feeler and the thinker work together on the campaign, each handling the part where their style will have the most impact; the feeler providing the message and the thinker planning the strategy, their chances of a dynamite response are multiplied. By allowing each other to manage a part of the campaign in their own style, they have created something else — something greater than either are capable of individually.

In other cases, one partner may be a strong planner while the other is spontaneous. By recognizing the value contained in each quality, a couple may create a management style that was well thought out but punctuated with excitement and adventure.

> *"Working together requires tremendous understanding between two people. Having different duties to be responsible for helps. I am a workhorse and my husband is the overall planner-marketer!"* Lily Vieyra, Eureka, CA

The most obvious advantage of combining management styles are when each partner excels in different qualities and can offset one another. When you are equally suited to a function, you may want to get creative. For example, if your business permits, you may share or take turns. In reverse, when you are equally unsuited (meaning you are unqualified, have no desire and no time) you may have to draw straws, hire someone or restructure the job.

Once you begin to see the possibilities of combining your differences instead of fighting against them, you will probably be excited to experience the effects.

In the beginning, working with a joint style can be threatening and uncomfortable. A few temporary rules can make the transition go more smoothly. After you have experienced the power of your new management style you won't need the rules anymore. Operating with your new style will be both a relief and a wonderment.

> *"We really are much closer than we used to be. But, I'm not sure why. It just happens! I do feel we have more respect for each other's qualities."* Sherry Shinn, Lee's Summit, MO

The Temporary Rules:

♦ **Release control over areas not assigned to you.** Your partner's capabilities have been proven. Stay involved and give input, but accept decisions made by your partner.

♦ **Respect your partner's strengths.** Be in awe of those things — no matter what they are, how big or how small — that your partner can do that you either have no talent for or don't like. Remember that without this contribution, your life and/or business would be harder or even lacking.

♦ **Stay involved with each other.** You are in this together. There should be no secrets and no job should be thought of as less of a contribution than another.

♦ **Forgive mistakes.** You will also make mistakes. It is part of why we are here.

Businesses and couples have everything to gain when differing styles are used to compliment rather than confront. For a small business to survive requires keeping pace with technology, in tune with the needs and demands of customers and constantly aware of changing trends and focus.

Two Heads Are Better Than One

> *"The greatest advantage of working together is two people performing as one; the whole being greater than the sum of it's parts." F.P., Flint, MI*

As a Couple at Work, you are equipped with a dual tool — two heads, two minds and two genders to approach the challenges of a rapidly changing society. Men and women have a lot to learn from each other and by *being receptive*, a lot to accomplish.

Sharon Nelton in "Men, Women and Leadership," *Nation's Business,* (May 1991) quotes Edward M. Moldt, Managing Director of the Snider Entrepreneurial Center, "Today's companies, require leaders who not only are risk-takers and visionaries but also are smart enough people that they're capable of hearing the ideas of others and really empowering them to use some of those ideas in changing businesses and in making them successful."

Sharon goes on to say that female leadership may be able to help companies solve the problems of better customer service, demand for higher quality and leadership itself. All require relationship-building skills in which women excel. Many men are learning how to incorporate these skills into their styles.

Speaking for what women can learn from men is Jim Autry, President of Meredith Corp. in Des Moines, IA. Autry says, "Consider being more decisive. This doesn't mean having a closed mind or being bullheaded." He suggests, "Decisiveness is an area that I think women could probably learn something from men about. Women often lack a sense of timing about when to stop building consensus and gathering information and to make a decision."

> *"Our management and work styles are different. It gives me balance to see the compliment for working with a masculine person to whom I am very attached."*
> *J.A.D., Aurora, CO*

The rewards come from being objectively aware of the value in each other and what's working and what isn't. Openly consider if you can benefit by learning and incorporating any of your partner's qualities into your own method without giving up yourself. Draw what you can from each other, but use only what is comfortable and comes across naturally.

When It Doesn't Work

Couples at Work who have overcome the obstacles of conflicts in management styles and come away feeling satisfied and closer, have done so with distinctive principles:

♦   They are determined to make it work.
♦   They feel that by working together their lives and accomplishments are fuller.
♦   They value and respect each other.
♦   They feel their partner makes a valuable contribution.
♦   They have relinquished controlling behavior and left their egos to lesser causes.

In some cases, the possession of these tools is timing, experience, pain, or pleasure. In other situations, one partner has no sincere interest in developing an equal partnership.

Another obstacle may be lack of knowledge or training in good management techniques. Whatever the reason, some partners have difficulty ever reaching a comfortable and happy understanding of each other's management style.

> *"You must be best friends and be willing to allow your partner creativity and not be overly critical of qualities you don't particularly like ." G.J.,Worcester, MA*

Before giving in to failure, try to get to the bottom of the conflict. Consider why there is a problem. Ask yourself a few questions and try to be honest and objective in your answers.

♦   Is the style that bothers you damaging the business or the relationship? Why? Name specific examples of damage that have resulted from the style you don't like.

♦   Is the style contrary to the situation? Is there an overlap in authority? Are you both working together because you want to?

◆   Are there power struggles and control issues dictating actions? Do one or the other of you insist on always having things done your way?

Next, consider if there are any steps you could initiate to solve the problem.

◆   Do you need to designate separate areas of responsibilities and authority and then commit to stay out of each other's territory? Should you have separate offices? Could part of the work be done somewhere else?

◆   Are some functions of your business more conducive to one style than another? Are they distributed so as to utilize each of your strengths to your advantage? Are they distributed fairly?

◆   Would training help? Books, workshops and classes are readily available through family business centers, firms, conferences, government agencies, public education, and special seminars and workshops.

> *"Working together has strengthened our marriage — it's like being on the same team and working towards the same goals."*
> *Karen Weiss, Tamarac, FL*

Don't be afraid to ask for help in this process. There are many family business counselors all over the country. Read the next chapter on conflict resolution. Business hours take up at least one third — and usually more — of your life. If it isn't working, it isn't worth the misery.

Dub

At the time, it was really irritating that Janet was taking so long to hire a salesman. In retrospect, I understand she had to find the right one because she and I had come up with a blueprint of where we were going and how we were going to get there. If we were serious, she was obligated to search until she found him.

In reality, it took a better salesman to work recycled product. He had to be creative. Unlike stores selling new furniture, we had no catalog, no consistent inventory and no pick-up or delivery service.

In the back of my mind, I really was grateful Janet was on the job. We saw the same big picture and the same end result. We just had two different routes to get there.

Once we figured it out, having Janet as the 'Thinker' and me as the 'Doer' was a dynamite combo. As she was organized, structured and patient (especially with me), I was building rapport with clients and customers. While she was building a foundation, I was building a showplace.

Once we stopped trying to change each other and learned to accept each other's style as having value, we were surprised to find out how much influence we had as a team.

Janet

Well, a few days later, I did hire a salesman. The salesman I got was everything we needed — experienced, personable, cooperative, and didn't let a customer leave without buying at least one more thing than they came in for. The wait had paid off.

I have to admit, I guess, that I may have continued interviewing and analyzing if Dub had not been so impatient. There's a saying that if you do something for twenty days in a row, it will become a habit. I was way beyond that timetable. On the other hand, if I'd succumbed to just 'getting a body,' I would have perpetuated the established history of 'troubled' salesmen. In this case, my patience and his impatience worked together to achieve exactly the results that we needed.

Although in the beginning I was uncomfortable with much of Dub's management style, as time went on I began to see how valuable our differences were to each other. While I offered organization and stability, he offered excitement and emotional involvement. Where I made people feel secure, he made them feel invested.

While I learned to take more risks, he learned to be more calculated. When I had an idea, he acted on it. We were the hare and the turtle — but he learned to be more balanced and I learned to be make decisions more quickly.

His comfort in the limelight was offset by my strength as a listener. His charisma with the public and business savvy were perfect for buying product, while my attention to detail and people skills were ideal for operations.

Together we were visionaries always looking at how what we did today would take us into tomorrow. We were beginning to see that as individuals we were catalysts to each other — that we were creating a third self, a powerful blend of ingredients that served to expand us both.

More Reading About Management Styles

Benfari, Robert, *Understanding Your Management Style,* Lexington Books, 1991.

Driver, Michael, *Dynamic Decision Making,* Jossey-Bass, 1993.

Hawkins, Kathleen L. and Turla, Peter A., *Test Your Entrepreneurial I.Q.,* Berkley Books, 1986.

Jeffries, William C., *True To Type,* Hampton Roads Publishing Co., Inc., 1991.

Johnson, Kerry L., *Building Your Management Skills,* Managers Magazine, July 1989.

Kroeger, Otto, *Type Talk At Work,* Delocorte Press,1992.

Sedgwick, Henry D., *To Thine Own Self Be True,* Inc, August 1994.

Sweed, Phyllis, *How Do You Manage?* (Editorial), Gift Shops Management, June 1993.

Wheeler, Carol, *Secrets of Top Managers,* Executive Female, May-June 1994.

Survey responses to the question *"When you were consider-ing working together, what issues most concerned you about combining your relationship with business?"*

> "I just didn't know if our temperaments could be together all day. He is quick to temper, fast to cool off. I'm calmer and more sensitive and get hurt feelings."
> Karen Weiss, Tamarack, FL.

> "We were both strong willed people going into a people business with very different styles of handling things."
> Christy Lacey-Igoe, Cape May, NJ

> "As well as having self-employed parents, I was self-employed in a former marriage. I understand the stress and commitment needed.
> Marilyn Ebel, Lancaster, PA

> "We were most concerned about the diminished time with the kids"
> Sherry Shinn, Lees's Summit, MO

> "He's the type that will do anything to please the next guy. I'm more limited. Also since this was really his business idea, I thought I would be more like his hired hand."
> H.H.,Rockford, IL

Survey responses *to the question "After you had been working together what turned out to be real problems?"*

"Sometimes stressful situations would lead to me being hurt or not appreciated."
Karen Weiss, Tamarack, FL

"Problems revolve around not making enough money to hire help. We're overworked!"
Sherry Shinn, Lee's Summit, MO

" The personality conflicts were a problem — also time off."
Christy Lacey-Igoe, Cape May, N.J.

"We get in each other's way sometimes. Communication tends to be a problem. Not enough free time and difficult to stay romantic when we are together so much."
Marilyn Sanko-Ebel, Lancaster, PA

"I am his hired hand — not much of a partner. We also have personality conficts and can't get enough time off.
H.H., Rockford, IL

Chapter 8
Cultivating Conflict

Dub

My relationship with Janet has taken me places I've never been before. They are places I didn't really want to go, but I'm glad I've been.

I grew up in a loving, kiss-and-hug-family where no one raised a voice in anger and rarely was an argument heard. I had not learned how to confront, question or voice my opinion. I thought what I was told to think and didn't really know what my own beliefs were.

When I met Janet, I had recently broken off a business relationship with my older sister and needed help evaluating a hotel property I was renovating. I called a temporary agency and it was Janet who came. She came into my life the day before Thanksgiving 1987.

It was love/lust at first sight. She was everything — and more — I had ever wanted in a woman. She was beautiful, smart and giving. The job lasted a couple of weeks and by the end we were in love. We knew we wanted to share the rest of our lives with each other.

The next few years were a continuous obstacle course. As much as we loved each other, we couldn't seem to get along. We needed someone to help us figure out what was going on and finally went to a therapist. Most of our conflict had nothing to do with each other; instead it was based on old fears and insecurities that had been hidden for so long.

It was all new to me. I had never been here in a relationship before and I just didn't understand what was going on.

I thought if this was the woman of my dreams, a match made in heaven, then there would be no conflict. It was supposed to be wonderful. She kept telling me over and over, 'to have a good relationship you have to work at it,' but this just seemed stupid.

Janet

Up until just a few years before I met Dub, I was a chronic conflict-avoider. The idea of confrontation was so threatening to me that any trade-off seemed like a better choice. I learned all the traditional escape tactics — leave, avoid and suppress.

I did my best to surround myself with people who thought like I did, appreciated my approach and supported my direction. I invited no criticism and offered no disagreement.

None of these things are bad — to a degree. Most of us choose our friends according to common interests and values. It's good to let petty things pass and be a positive influence in the lives of those around us.

The problem arises when the price of being 'nice' is losing yourself because you are afraid to express opposing beliefs and opinions, when anger and resentment override happiness and love. When the price includes choosing to be alone because you don't feel 'safe' with other people, you've lost the balance.

In business, it was different. When conflict arose, I handled it — it was business and that's what was expected of me and that's what I expected of myself.

Fortunately, before I got too deep in the hole I was digging, I met a lady who quickly became a steadfast friend. When we first met, our friendship was glued together by the fact that we were both going through a divorce. Our backgrounds were so different that in many ways we had nothing in common. She was a military wife, a teacher and had traveled around the world. I was living in the mountains, shoveling snow and building my career.

After our divorce woes subsided, we had almost no choice but to continue the friendship. We had shared so much of ourselves with each other that we had become close. A few years later, we became roommates and business partners. Our lives were so entwined that we could not avoid the usual bumps and grinds of close relationships. And because we were in business together, I had to voice my opinions.

What happened in this relationship changed my life. She never judged me, rejected me or told me I was wrong when I confronted her. Instead, she listened to what I said, weighed it and then either credited me with my observation or explained her position.

The outcome caught me completely off guard. It was so rewarding and so releasing to express myself honestly, and it made our friendship stronger. She taught me, through her response, that it was not only okay to disagree, it was advantageous.

By the time I met Dub, conflict in caring relationships had taken on new meaning for me. It meant growth, enhanced inti-

macy and the freedom to be myself.

Poor Dub. He didn't know what hit him.

What Is This Thing Called Conflict?

What is it about the word conflict that makes grown people cower, turn away or run like the wind when it arises in their relationships? Why do normal people who daily confront and solve conflicts in business react with shock, sadness, disappointment, and even disgust when confronted by a disagreement with their mate?

> *"Some people quit as soon as things (jobs, relationships) have problems instead of noticing that NOTHING is perfect and trying to work through it."* Tamela S. Kenning, Ouray, CO

Where did the idea originate that if you're meant to be together with a certain person you will live in harmony forever? Where does the hopelessness come from when disagreements arise?

Put a Couple at Work in the mixer and the potential for conflict is enormous. Contributing factors go beyond the normal ones people face. Differences in gender, money attitudes, and personality are supplemented with management styles, employees, customers, schedules, and business stress.

By taking a closer look, the idea of conflict is not nearly as powerful as the feelings that arise from it. The feelings are unpleasant, sometimes unnerving; and although often represent a level of fear, may be projected as anger, depression aggressive behavior, or rebellion.

In an intimate relationship where each member is vulnerable these feelings are intensified. This is perhaps one explanation of why conflict in personal settings is so unacceptable.

The first reaction is usually to blame someone for creating the feeling, and the second reaction is to escape. Escape comes in a variety of forms, such as clamming up, ignoring the issue, leaving, or inventing distractions.

Countless experts have studied couples and conflict and have devised a number of techniques for working through them. At the heart of them is getting inside you and your beliefs — how does this struggle make you feel about yourself and why?

Although you can approach conflict resolution at any stage in your relationship, it may be helpful to first accept and even welcome these seemingly undesirable scenarios into your relationship. Of course that may mean a real shift in your familiar and comfortable perspective.

Changing The Way You See Conflict

As a Couple at Work, you have a natural platform for insisting you deal with issues quickly, productively and without too much commotion. Customers, employees, deadlines, and production are dependent on how you react.

> *"Conflicts at home carry over to work and conflicts at work carry into the home. There is no 'time-out' and everyone around is affected."* Tamela Kenning, Ouray, CO

Learning how to resolve your differences in the workplace offers not only a speedy solution to business issues, but will spill over into your personal life.

To reach this level of compatibility, you must develop understanding that conflict is natural, expect it to occur and then redefine it. The key to success is not eliminating dissension but learning how to deal with it. This is not an easy assignment. Accept that it will take many attempts and experiences before such a major shift will stick.

Begin by asking yourself what words or associations pop into your mind when you think of conflict. If they are such things as win/lose, fight, power, war, destruction, control, mistake, or any negative definition, you have begun to understand why you might want to avoid dealing with conflict. By fearing conflict you may be destroying your chances to deal with it effectively.

To experiment with a new perspective of conflict, try giving it new associations. Play with ideas like challenging, stimulating and diversifying. Imagine that every conflict contains a seed of potential growth, alternative thinking, opportunities to experience life more fully, and a catalyst for strengthening your relationship.

Stretch your imagination. Try to believe that conflict can clarify your relationship rather than separate it. Forget about winning and losing. Think about growing and inventing new ways to behave.

Consider that opposites attract. Why is that?

Imagine you have selected your partner because deep inside you knew this person, who is so different from you, has the ability to transform you in some way.

John Welwood in an article for *New Age* Magazine, (July/ August 1996), suggests that there are two reasons we are drawn to certain partners. One, that we have a "heart connection," meaning that we feel full and nourished, the feeling often associated when first falling in love. The second draw is a "soul connection," a deep seated tug from a deeper level. He says that certain people recognize and love us in another dimension. Their by the facades we have worked so hard to develop for survival. These people see through the lines we use to get what we want

— the lines we use so often, we believe them. They question us about our motives and meaning, and unwittingly force us to the truth.

In other words, sometimes we seem to be magically drawn to certain people who challenge the way we think or perceive things. While they may seem argumentative, uncooperative or even hostile, they are actually helping us to break up the self-inflicted barriers that prevent us from evolving into more loving and accepting people.

As human beings often resistant to change, this process usually seems contrary to what we expect in intimate relationships. In fact, it could be called conflict.

It helps to believe that your partner wants peace as much as you do and that most conflicts are seeded by good intentions rather than intentional jabs to make you feel bad. Remind yourselves that you are partners, not adversaries, and that differences are an opportunity to learn more about yourself and each other.

As a Couple at Work, you have still another opportunity to create a third, more powerful response to your business dilemmas. Compromising is not even required. Your goal is to reach a new, mutually satisfying — commonly known as a win/win — solution.

Is It Possible To See Conflict As Good?

Talking about getting a different perspective is a lot like planting a garden. It's easy to plant seeds, but if you don't put some energy into making them grow, not much will happen. You've got to water them, fertilize them and pull out a lot of weeds. Some days are too hot, some too cold and some days you have to get someone to help you with the job.

> *"Our relationship is strengthened by conflict. This didn't happen overnight. I wouldn't change the conflicts or the resolution or the opportunity for growth."*
> *E.N., Wilmington, DE*

Believing that conflict is a positive force in your life will only take root if you *experience* some benefits. Confronting your partner with your feelings is the first step. But in order to get positive results, you have to learn what works in your particular situation, how to approach your partner and how to react.

Before trying techniques to resolve your differences, you will need two essential ingredients.

Trust: You must agree to listen and accept each other's feelings and perspectives without judgement — a difficult task until it's your turn.

In Stephen Covey's book, *The 7 Habits of Highly Effective People,* he talks about an "emotional bank." The bank is used to make deposits of courtesy, kindness, honesty, and keeping commitments. By doing this, a reserve of trust is built which creates a safe environment for communicating, and even making mistakes. Trust is not a given in a relationship, it is earned.

Willingness: To effectively listen you have to release any determination to be right. If you are stuck on doing things your way, focusing on negative behavior or preparing your response instead of listening to what your partner is saying, you are not sincerely interested in mutual satisfaction.

Bring suggestions rather than solutions to the table. Your focus is on understanding and reaching a decision that is best for both of you and your business.

How Should You Begin?

Now that you have set the scene with the right frame of mind to welcome conflict, and you have promised trust and willingness, you are ready to begin.

A Couple at Work rarely has the luxury of settling disputes on the spot. In fact, many disagreements arise from decisions or commitments made by one partner without consideration of the other. If a precedent is set and the issue goes unresolved or misunderstood, resentment is fueled and eventually filters through to other areas.

Many couples in our survey say tension is experienced by everyone around them when they have disagreements, and they have no personal space or time in which to process their feelings. Unresolved issues in any circumstance are not going to go away.

> *"Whatever the issue, solve it that day!"*
> *Vic Mangini, Greenfield, N.H.*

For these couples, an agreement to set aside a time and place for discussion is a primary requirement for successful resolution. Knowing that an opportunity for communicating is pending often supplies immediate relief.

◆ ***Time and place***: Choose a time when interruptions will be minimal. Consider that the process requires energy, so don't plan it after a stressful meeting or when you know you are too tired.

   A place that is comfortable, and not distracting to both of you, will enhance your feelings of openness and ease.

◆ ***Review your approach:*** Discuss and agree how you will proceed so you each know what to expect. Will you each speak for five minutes uninterrupted? Will you follow the flow of natural conversation? Who will begin? Will you write difficult comments on paper? Do you expect feedback? Will you present suggestions for resolution?

> *"Highly emotional confrontations are modified by taking a position in writing."*
> Vic Mangini, Greenfield, N.H.

Repeat your willingness to be open and non-judgmental while listening to each other.

In *The Eight Essential Steps to Conflict Resolution,* Dudley Weeks, Ph.D., suggests an opening statement. It could go something like this, "I know we both have strong opinions and feelings about our situation, and I want you to know I will try to listen to and understand your point of view. I see us as needing each other to work through this particular conflict to help our relationship grow."

◆ *State your case:* Describe how the situation makes you feel and why. Does it make you feel responsible, lonely, burdened, left out, invalidated, unimportant, incompetent, unwanted, or insecure? Does your feeling remind you of something you experienced in the past? What is the same? What is different?

Practice effective communication skills, being careful not to criticize, attack or make demands. Start your sentences saying "I feel..." instead of "You make me feel..." Ask your partner to repeat what you said. Adjust any misperceptions. Use different words if necessary.

If you are the listener, be active. Ask questions to encourage the speaker and to clarify your understanding. If you are unsure of a meaning, ask your partner for more information. Don't take anything personally. It is not about you; it is about your partner's feelings on the subject. Your job is to support and accept without judgement.

Trade places and repeat the process.

♦ *State your needs:* What do you need to happen — not want, but need? Why is this a need? Do you have a deadline that can only be met if certain things occur? Will you lose a major account?

Will your reputation, credibility or authority be destroyed unless specific changes are made? Will trust be lost, or the relationship injured in some way?

Sometimes all you need is to get a grievance off your chest. Tell you partner that no action or response is required.

♦ *Present possible solutions*: With each solution, consider how the feelings of each partner will be affected and if each of your needs will be met. Can a slight adjustment make a big difference? Can you combine components from each of your suggestions to make a new solution? Should you start from scratch and come up with a completely new solution together?

Sometimes there are no solutions. You both may feel so strongly about your position that there is no room for new ground. Try to accept that these occasions will arise and you are both entitled to your viewpoint. If it is a constant in your relationship, you may have to take more serious action.

♦ *Make a commitment:* Once you have arrived at an agreeable direction, it is important to discuss how and when you will implement it. This serves to seal your commitment and clears up any ragged-edged misunderstandings.

♦ ***Forgive mistakes***: Everybody makes mistakes. If you haven't yet, you will. As a Couple at Work, it is essential to put things behind you and move forward.

When you are in a position to be forgiving, remember how difficult it is to forgive yourself when you have made a bad decision or said something you regret. No one feels worse than you. It is sometimes harder to forgive yourself than it is to forgive someone else.

"To carry an anger against anyone is to poison your own heart, administering more toxin every time you replay in your mind the injury done to you." says Patrick Miller in *A Little Book of Forgiveness,* Viking 1994.

> *"We have constantly improved our working-together skills. We have mutual respect for each other!"* Bill Stinson, Waitsfield, VT

Couples who are adept at this process can sometimes complete all the steps in a matter of seconds, especially for minor issues. Many of the Couples at Work in our survey say they have learned to let go of petty issues; they have learned how to evaluate what is important and what is not.

Even in the beginning, spending too much time trying to resolve something may do more harm than good. If you get stuck or angry and get off the track for too long, it may be a good idea to call it off temporarily until you have a chance to get back in control and try again.

Fighting In Style

Although few experts would argue about getting to the underlying feelings in most conflicts, there is evidence that some couples have differing techniques for successful resolution. In an article written for *Psych Today,* (March/April 1994), John

Gottman says that even fighting, when it airs grievances and complaints, "can be one of the healthiest things a couple can do for their relationship."

For 20 years, Mr. Gottman studied the marital relationships of over 200 couples and concluded that successful couples, no matter what their fighting style, all displayed plenty of positive strokes toward one another. Compliments, touching smiling and laughing were top priorities. He found that the magic balance was five positives to one negative. In other words, to offset every criticism or harsh word, five acts of love or support were given.

Couples, he said, settled into three distinct groups of problem solving.

◆ **Validating:** The couples in this group tended to address their differences before they felt angry or resentful. Their emphasis was on communication and compromise.

They displayed a lot of natural skill in listening and understanding each other's emotions. During the disagreement they regularly supported each other, validating their emotions, although still disagreeing. Mutual respect was strong.

◆ **Conflict-avoiding:** In this group couples rarely confronted their differences. Their understanding of marriage was to agree to disagree at times. Differences were not threatening nor did they call for confrontation. They preferred to work things out alone, often through a physical activity such as jogging.

◆ **Volatile:** This group contained couples who were very independent and who felt that marriage should strengthen their individuality. They considered themselves equal and their confrontations were frequent and intense.

Being open about their feelings, both negative and positive, was a given. In their exchanges, they frequently interrupted each other and defended themselves rather than listening to their partner. Their arguing was passionate but so was their making up. Excitement and even a hint of danger prevailed in these relationships.

> *"Even though I can let things fester, I do like to get things resolved. I don't like to let them linger on and on."* C.W.N., N. Conway, NH

Although the Validating couples use the most recommended approach for conflict resolution, the other two groups have proven that different people are receptive to varying techniques, an important factor in considering what works best for you.

When Conflict Never Gets Resolved

Your feelings and actions are the best measure of your conflict-resolution health. If you are often sad, depressed and feel lonely; if you have hidden agendas and behave in ways that you know hurt your partner, you are probably not satisfied with the outcome of your disagreements.

If you find that your relationship is deteriorating through criticism, contempt, defensiveness, and lack of communication, it is wise to enlist the help of a third person. As a Couple at Work, you cannot afford to carry around hostile feelings and behaviors.

With the immense growth and visibility of family business, home business and entrepreneurial ventures, a new breed of consultants is appearing to help solve common conflicts. Known as family business doctors, consultants and even virtual coaches who work through online services, fax and telephones, they are there to help families resolve issues about compensation, benefits, business and family priorities, communication, and many other matters.

> "Our relationship works because, in addition
> to being married, we are best friends. Under-
> standing a friend is different than understanding
> a spouse. Accordingly, we have a broader
> base on which to stand." *G.W., Dearborn, MI*

Couples that make working together a successful experience say they are best friends. This means accepting — not necessarily agreeing with — each other on every level. It means letting go of the need to control each other or feel superior. The more you listen, the more you can understand what the other person is trying to say.

Expecting to have differences with the people we love most in life was not something we were taught in school. Neither was learning how to turn those differences into assets. Don't expect to know. Expect the differences and learn how to expand your life with them. Be patient with the process, yourself and your partner. You have a lot to gain.

Dub

Working on complex conflict issues when you're not living with someone is one thing — but living and working together is something else. There is no more walking away. We had to sit down and work it out. We also had to decide what was worth getting upset about and what wasn't.

In the summer of '96, I read an article from New Age Journal, "Fighting for Enlightenment" by John Welwood. To paraphrase, John says we are often paired up with a mate that helps us break down those walls that keep us from being ourselves.

Janet had been breaking down my walls since 1987, but I guess I wasn't ready to give them up then. Now, when I get upset — and not just with Janet — I ask myself, 'What part of this is making me so angry and why?' The answer that usually comes up has little to do with the situation, but instead is a shadow of some unresolved issue of the past.

Janet and I still have disagreements, probably always will, but we seem to get along a lot better these days.

Janet

Although the first five years of our relationship were charged with mind-bending challenges, they also provided the catalyst we needed to propel ourselves into the next phase of our lives.

The intensity of our feelings for one another wouldn't allow us to stay stuck with selfish ideas and perceptions. Because we knew in our hearts that we wanted to be together, we were forced to stop being 'right,' open our minds and listen to each other.

Learning to listen without judgement and being open to trying new approaches is sometimes intimidating and sometimes impossible. For me, taking the chance has been worth it. I got to experience a whole new world.

Besides, I guess Dub is never going to be just like me!

More Reading About Conflict

Aronoff, Craig E. and Ward, John L., *Managing Family-Business Conflicts,* Nations's Business, November 1995.

Gottman, John, *What Makes Marriage Work?,* Psychology Today, March 1994.

Gray, John, *What You Can Feel, You Can Heal,*Heart Publishing Co., 1984.

Klaes, Jim, *Entrepreneurs Face "Field of Dreams,"* The University of Texas at El Paso College of Business Administration, September 1996.

Markman, Howard, *Six Truths for Couples,* Psychology Today, January 1994.

Nelton, Sharon, *The Power of Forgiveness,* Nations's Business, July 1995.

Week, Dudley, *The Eight Essesntial Steps to Conflict Resolution,* J.P. Tarcher, 1992.

Welwood, John, *Fighting for Enlightenment,* New Age Journal, July/August 1996.

Vinton, Karen L., *Business — In Crisis,* case study, U.S. Chamber of Commerce, 1995.

Survey responses to the question "If conflict strengthens your relationship as a result of working together, what BEST explains the reason?"

"We spend time trying to see each other's point of view."
Kathy Larson, Sandy, UT

"We have found we can be more sympathetic and compassionate on issues."
Sherry Shinn, Lee's Summit, MO

And "...if conflict divides your relationship?"

"Misunderstanding in communication (poor communication skills at times)."
R.C.P., Pikeville, TN

"I am very sensitive and often take criticism personally."
M.D., El Paso, TX

Survey responses *to the question "When conflicts arise, how would you say they are handled?"*

"Resolutions are reached quickly, but not always happily."
G.D., Flagstaff, AZ

"In the beginning two years everyone knew we were having problems. Steam seemed to come off both of us."
Christy Lacey-Igoe, Cape May, NJ

"Our relationship is strengthened — afterwards — when we sit down and review the situation." William Ebel, Jr. Lancster, PA

"We don't have any conflicts."
Arch Edwards, Edenton, NC

"Conflict is not part of my life."
Jane Edwards, Edenton, NC

"After discussion — issues are resolved."
Karen Weiss, Tamarac, FL

Chapter 9
Getting Time Off — From Work And Each Other

Dub

I've always thought the best way to tell if you practice good management is to see how well a business runs without you. I don't know if I was ever self-confident enough to deliberately test that notion.

I had often envied people who could take an afternoon to play golf or go to a movie. At the same time, I couldn't understand how they could be so irresponsible. In my mind, as long as there's light outside and the clock is somewhere between eight and five, you should work, not play. Some opportunity might come and go and you wouldn't be there.

Maybe this attitude explains why I've never had any balance in my life, but two and a half years in this business and no vacation was much too long. One morning early in April, a buddy of mine called to see if Janet and I would be interested in a trip to the Virgin Islands. Could I do it?

Janet

I desperately needed a vacation. In a year's time my life had changed from a nicely balanced arrangement of work and play to an obsessive focus on business. While working the 24 hour day, seven days a week theory, my roaming side was under-nourished and starved for attention. Apart from one evening a week with a girlfriend, my life was entirely spent with the business and/or with Dub.

We were inseparable, partly because of necessity, partly because our working and living together had born a sort of dependency on each other that kept begging for more. Our lives were so entwined that to break away for even a few hours was almost a violation of some unspoken law. We had become committed to each other and to making the business successful.

But I missed my friends, family, those spontaneous weekend getaways to the ocean or mountains, and the always-pending trip to some exotic place. I knew our life was out of balance, but accepted that fact, for the time being, because we had chosen to devote our lives to developing a solid foundation for our future.

And then we got the invitation to charter a yacht in the Virgin Islands with another couple. It meant being gone for three weeks. I knew Dub would never go for it...

Exactly How Important Is Time Off?

Getting personal time away from the business and sometimes each other is, according to our survey, the number one difficulty for couples that work together. Finding a way to let go of the business and turn it over to someone trustworthy and competent, seems to be a major challenge.

And yet studies show that those who live the most fulfilling lives are those who help themselves to healthy servings of play.

Apparently, these people realize that by nurturing themselves, they are able to not only nurture others, but bring fresh energy to making their businesses soar.

Frequently in the start-up stages of a small business, nobody else can handle things. Employees haven't become vested in loyalty and knowledge, customers are being cultivated, operations and routines are still being defined and there are too many surprises with no precedent procedures.

The length of time it takes to get established and secure varies by business, but at some point that stage settles into a more manageable one. If chaos prevails permanently, there are other things going on that are too big to be addressed in this book. Ultimately, *taking time off is simply a decision.*

> *"There are boundaries and limits. My husband and my well-being must have some priority. I will no longer be OWNED by work."*
> A.J., Olympia, WA

Introducing thoughts and activities that are unlike your usual focus is what taking time off is all about. Even if you love what you do, a break or change of pace is revitalizing and illuminating. Fresh enthusiasm and team-building patience are rewards of even the smallest of getaways. Your mind and body need rest, need food and perform much better if nourished.

Although a break from the business can be long and noticeable, it doesn't have to be. It does have to be something you really enjoy.

It might mean taking two hours in the middle of the day and watching a movie by yourself in the silence of your home. Maybe it's going to an exercise class at 10 a.m., sitting in the park quietly for 45 minutes, or listening to music in your car.

Planning Your Time Off

How you manage your time depends on knowing *where you are going*. What does that mean?

It's easy, and even necessary, to make your To Do List for the day, the week and the month of all the projects, appointments and other commitments you have. It's easy because you have a pretty good idea what results you expect — a new client, completed training, increased visibility, a signed contract, more inventory, etc. And, you have a good idea of what you need to do to get those results.

What if you made a To Do List for your *life*? List all the results you want to end up with and the actions necessary to accomplish them. Suppose the results on your list looked something like this.

♦ Have the freedom to move around as I please, living or traveling wherever I want, whenever I want.

♦ Be healthy, fit and active.

♦ Have loving, healthy relationships with my family members.

♦ Be spiritually connected with a sense of purpose and direction.

♦ Be a contributing member of society, influencing in my own special way.

♦ Spend my work time on activities that give me a sense of excitement, growth and accomplishment.

♦ Have full and satisfying relationships with friends and

associates.

◆ Be interesting and interested.

Where are the homes, the boats, the multi-million dollar businesses you ask? Be patient — you can have those too if you want, but is that the first priority? If you have no one to share them with, you are a physical wreck and nobody likes you, do they still matter?

> *"Who cares if the business works if you don't get along? " Mark Pitts, Union Pier, MI*

Before going further with your life list, how does it compare to a list of long term results you may have made for your business? An example could look something like this.

◆ Have two locations.

◆ Earn net income of $60,000 annually.

◆ Be well known in the community.

◆ Be recognized as having the best product in the country.

◆ Provide excellent customer service.

◆ Have trained employees.

◆ Provide quality service and competitive pricing.

◆ Provides legacy to family.

A well run business will have a specific plan to achieve these goals. Maybe the second location will be opened in three years, and in order for that to occur annual gross sales need to be half a million dollars.

The plan would then outline ways to meet that revenue requirement. Much of the revenue may be dependent on well trained employees, building a good reputation, offering a good product at the right price, and networking in the community.

Although more emphasis may be placed on one particular activity at any given time — say prospecting for new clients, all must be addressed to some degree simultaneously to achieve the desired results. Although training may be a primary focus for six months, marketing and product development cannot be overlooked.

> *"Having limits is one of the reasons for being self-employed."* J.P., Rockport, MA

In your To Do List for life, the same principles apply. While building your business may help achieve the freedom mentioned on your life list, you cannot ignore the things you must do to end up with rewarding relationships, physical health, and peace of mind. As in business, some items on your To Do List will require front stage for a period of time, but the others cannot be ignored if you are to ultimately realize the quality of life you want.

That's easy enough to understand. So why is getting time off such a problem? It's a problem because nobody got out the map to find out where you're going. Once you get your results for life clearly in your mind, you are going to put those activities that lead you there on your To Do List along with your business activities.

Because you want to be fit and healthy, you are going to ask yourself what you can do to promote that goal. You are going to find out what things affect your health, what you can do to implement positive input and you are going to put them on your list.

If it means reducing fat in your diet, you are going to buy low fat products; if it means exercise and you don't get enough on your job, you are going to put some time for it on your schedule every day or at least three times a week. If it means reducing stress, you are going to learn to meditate, breath deeply, listen to music, get a massage, shut your door and close your eyes, or whatever works for you.

Because you want to have healthy, loving relationships, you are going to find out what it takes to have them and you are going to be willing to learn about yourself, get rid of things that stand in the way of your progress and introduce changes when you realize the potential benefits of those changes.

You are going to find ways to relate to your partner, your children, your parents and you are going to find moments to do simple things that make big differences.

Because you want to be interesting you are going to be a sponge for learning new things. You will find what ways work best for you, whether it is talking to people, going places that are new or even strange to you, watching documentaries or reading books. Because you have openly and consciously acknowledged this goal, you will be constantly attuned for anything that helps you get there.

> *"Sometime you have to catch your breath and realize that there's more going on here than just work."* G.O., Atherton, CA

If you take the time to genuinely discover where you want to go with your life, the results on your list will become part of your daily consciousness. Many things take years, even lifetimes to accomplish. You can't start working on them when you are ready to have them. Therefore, you must develop the mentality to include all these things in your life as soon as possible.

In the movie, *Wrestling Ernest Hemingway,* two old men, Frank and Walter, are discussing why Walter never had a wife and family. Walter says "I had to build my barber business. Then suddenly, I was an old man." He was sad, lonely and stuck in his routine. His life energy had been spent developing a successful barbershop. His needs of closeness and human interaction had been traded for a few years of worldly success.

Frank was lonely too. His son acknowledged his birthday with an empty promise to visit and a stupid hat because all he knew about his father was his playful, antic-driven behavior. He didn't know how desperately Frank wanted to see him or how much he counted on his visits.

Frank hadn't invested in the end result of being close to his son. As an old man he continued to act immaturely, drinking too much and distracting himself from his feelings of abandonment and emptiness.

Walter and Frank got to their destination, but nothing was there.

Is That The Alarm?

Could it be that Couples at Work who say they can't get enough time off are really saying that other parts of them are being neglected? Are their internal alarms going off?

> *"The stress of being a business owner, a parent and an involved community member have compromised my health. I've started taking an hour or more per day for myself to do stress reduction things and things I like."*
> *C.W.N., N. Conway, NH*

Have their needs to develop more closeness with their mates and children, interact with friends, be stimulated by new ideas, other worlds, to find more meaning in life, to rest and relax, and to get to know and feel good about themselves, been shoved on the back burner for too long? Is it more about *feeling* differently than time off itself?

By developing your life list of results and believing that you must act now to promote them, you have made them a priority along with the goals you have set for your business. Your normal To Do List, whether it is on paper or in your head, will automatically include some activity to direct you. It may be something as simple as calling your dad, taking 30 minutes with your five year old to color, listening to an inspirational tape, or having lunch with a friend. But things will consistently appear on your list and they will consistently have an impact.

As a Couple at Work, there are many practical things you can do to assure your life does not get permanently out of balance, that you give attention to your personal needs as well as your long-range results.

First, determine what you ultimately want and what you need to do to get it. Understand that, like a business, it often takes many years to achieve your results. There are often lessons to learn, techniques to master, obstacles to overcome, detours, and sometimes uncontrollable circumstances. Know too that there will be pleasure along the way.

And finally, *make the decision* to give time to yourself and your future. Expect some things to be forgotten for periods of time as others take precedence and be open to changing your expectations and desires as you evolve. With your higher thinking you can implement many of the time management principles with ease.

Getting The Time You Need

Couples at Work have all the usual problems of trying to find enough time for all the demands of the business, running a household, maintaining and developing relationships with family and friends, and nourishing and improving themselves. They have an additional challenge of finding time to keep their relationship fresh, stimulating and romantic after being together all day in a stressful work environment.

> *"People need to be partners at home as well as business."* D.A., Racine, WI

According to Harriet Schechter and Vicki T. Gibbs, co-authors of *More Time for Sex,* life is compromised 90 percent of maintenance activities. Maintenance at home includes such things as vehicle upkeep, cooking, paying bills, trash disposal, gardening, running errands, seasonal demands, and so forth. At work, it might be things like answering phones, responding to correspondence, filing, paying bills, reading publications, attending to employees or customers, opening and closing, etc.

The remaining 10 percent of time is available for special projects, which at home may be cleaning out the garage or re-arranging the furniture, and at work, setting up a filing system or developing a seminar. If this is true, it becomes quite clear why never having enough time to do important things is a chronic complaint.

The fact is, the maintenance activities are what give us the impetus to tackle the project time. Without clean clothes, food and running cars we may not have the appearance, energy or ability to proceed beyond our simple existence. And without happy customers, employees or communication, there may be no need for seminars or filing systems.

Maybe these details that we so resent should be given a little more respect. The key is twofold: figure out which ones you can do without and get the rest organized. For a Couple at Work, a mutual understanding of their importance and an agreeable method of achieving them is essential.

Business: Refer to your life list. What qualities do you want that may be related to running your business more efficiently and what can you be doing now?

> *"Business dictates our lifestyle."*
> *A.T., Tyler, TX*

After your business has passed the critical start-up stage, you can adjust your focus to include other elements in your life. This will take a little planning but will go a long way in creating a more balanced and pleasing lifestyle.

◆   ***Delegation:*** If you have employees, you have a great substitute for yourself if you are willing to let go of the belief that your business will collapse without you.

Maybe you fear letting go because you know deep down you aren't as indispensable as you'd like to think. Do you fear that by allowing others to represent you, you will lose respect or control and be permanently displaced?

If you are exhausted, burnt out or aching for time off, you may want to rethink this. Your company may be better served if you spend your time planning and implementing strategies that increase revenue or productivity rather than doing everything.

To assure that employees are loyal, have the ability to make decisions as you would and carry on to your benefit in your absence, you will have to train them well, reward and support them, give them responsibility and authority, make them accountable, share your company philosophy, help them see the big picture and whatever else it takes for your particular situation.

Begin with routine tasks and as they are proven, add

more demanding tasks and eventually leave them alone for short periods to build confidence for both you and them. As trust and assurance build, you will be able to leave for longer periods, and eventually take vacations.

If your business and long term goals permit, hire a manager.

◆ ***Prioritizing***: Whether or not you have employees, you can get more time by prioritizing your work. It is a rare situation where every task is top priority. Maybe your list is full of urgent items that you *want* to do, not items that will make or break your business.

Learn how to make top priority items ones that will pay off in free time or less responsibility later. For example, spend a week learning a software program that will simplify accounting, design, tracking sales, presentations, etc. Although the initial expense of learning is time consuming, the rewards are abundant.

> *"Take time when you can.*
> *Plan time in advance and*
> *then work around it."*
> *F.O., Palm Springs, CA*

◆ ***Seasonal planning:*** Most businesses have slow periods. These are especially important to acknowledge for Couples at Work without employees. Put these on your calendar and plan a getaway well in advance. Close up shop if you can.

If the slow season is the time you catch up on low priority items, go ahead and schedule a few days for that too. But if they haven't been done for a long time, how much difference will it make if they go undone compared to the rejuvenation you may feel from getting a change of scenery?

◆ ***Organizing:*** Plan, plan, plan. Scan your To Do List for the day or week highlighting the items that will make the most impact in your accomplishments and noting which are optional.

Set aside small jobs that can be squeezed in or combined with other activities. For example, you may enjoy reading a trade journal over lunch. At the same time, you may be reviewing it for information to be included in a speech you are delivering.

Big projects, especially unpleasant or unclear ones, should be broken down and tackled in little segments. Doing one small thing, like arranging all the information in a neat pile, generates amazing feelings of accomplishment.

If you have errands to run, map out your itinerary and prepare any materials you may need to take with you. Running around in circles and forgetting important items is not only a time-waster, but highly stressful.

Plan to wait. If you go to the bank, the doctor or even to lunch, there will very possibly be a significant chunk of waiting time that you could use to scan memos, research materials, even think about a particular situation. If you plan to wait, you will reduce the amount of energy you spend being irritated.

Another good opportunity for simple accomplishments is when you are waiting on the phone. Draft key points for letters, break down a big project, write short notes, make some notes for a brochure or seminar.

Interruptions are a given in business so plan for them. They may even be the reason for your business. Like waiting, expecting interruptions can be tolerated, and even welcomed.

Depending on your business, you may be able to schedule customers, employees and even phone calls at certain times, preserving other times for your full concentration on other things. The idea is to control your business; not to let your business control you.

Take a few minutes every day when things are fresh in your mind to review what has occurred and position yourself for the next days' activities.

Plan meetings around their purpose, i.e. relay information, gather input, instruct or negotiate. Keep the time appropriate with the purpose and limit off-subject interruptions. Do not feel that meetings must always be formal, sit-down affairs. For some meetings a 30-second gathering around the coffee pot produces the desired result.

Household: Is there anything on your life list that maybe effected by how you handle your responsibilities on the home front?

Household chores don't go away but some of them can be sacrificed or at least compromised.

◆   *Divide up and shut up:* Most household chores can be broken into several main categories and if you're having problems in this area, you may want to chart them out and take a look at whose doing what.

The major areas are the kitchen, bedrooms, cleaning, laundry, errands, trash, pets, home office and seasonal chores. For a thorough breakdown see the Schechter and Gibbs book mentioned earlier.

> *"Understand that it's okay to do things differently — whether style in setting table, decorating rooms, what combination of foods to serve. It may be done 'his way' one day and mine another."* R.O., Abilene, TX

If you are going to agree to divide up the chores, you also need to agree to release your standard of doing the chore. In other words, if you only make the bed with hospital corners and your partner who is assigned to that chore just pulls up the covers and lets the corners hang down, you either have to live with that, or do the chore yourself without complaint.

One way to beat the meal preparation dilemma is to cook many meals in one day and freeze them. Some couples like to prepare meals together and talk about their day as they work. For other couples, cooking is therapeutic and provides a period to unwind.

Other couples say they eat out all the time, and eating at home is a special event. Some use crock pots, timers or microwaves, preparing the meal in the morning when it doesn't seem like such a burden, and others get their children to help.

If you can't reach an equitable balance in doing household chores, one of you may take a day or an afternoon away from work. If neither of you wants to do them, hire someone to come in either regularly or periodically.

Family time: Review your life list. Do family relationships have any part of your future? If so, you better get clear about that now, because you only have a temporary window of time to work on it.

> *"Spend as much time with your children as you can because they are soon gone; family is more important than professions or any business."* C.G., Rochester, NY

If your children are school-age or younger, you, as a Couple at Work, have opportunities that employed people don't have. Your schedule can be flexed to attend their functions, stay home when they are sick, bring them to work if your business permits, and take turns playing taxi. They can bring their homework to the office, you can oversee them, even have them help you with small tasks.

♦ **Set aside time:** Put being together with your children on your schedule. Be sure it is undistracted time where you can get into their heads and find out who they are and what they like. Take half an hour and play a computer game, basketball, dolls, or whatever they want. Take them to lunch or go for an ice cream. Listen to them with your full attention. It doesn't take a lot of time — it takes a lot of involvement.

♦ **Be spontaneous**: Watch for opportunities when you can grab a few minutes together and make it count. Maybe they need a 15 minute ride to an activity. Take a few minutes when they go to bed and ask them how their day went. If they're making a milkshake, go make it with them.

♦ **Take turns:** If you both can't go to their school functions, sports events or other activities, take turns going. It's important that you both be involved in their lives. Make some days family days — go for picnics, cross country skiing, fishing, or just hang around together. Have all your meals at home and watch a football game, go to church, shop or play games.

The only way you will have family time is to *recognize the fleeting quality* of your opportunity to do so.

Self development/enrichment: What is on your life list that can be influenced if you pay attention to your personal growth?

> *"I never have time to myself — I am a musician and a writer. My creativity has suffered because of working so much. Also I don't have time to practice these skills."*
> Sally Krueger, Flagstaff, AZ

In the *Ninety-Minute Hour,* Jay Conrad Levinson describes an approach to doing two things at once, thus making your time doubly valuable. Obviously, there are certain activities that require full focus and would not qualify for this method.

◆ *Identify available time:* Check your day and consider all the activities that have some degree of waiting or "available time." Include driving, cooking, shaving, putting on make-up, walking, exercising, or sitting on an airplane, train or bus. All of these require selective concentration. While you are doing them you can receive input from a variety of other sources including tapes, VCRs, computers with multi media capability, television, and radio.

◆ *Input from tapes:* Tapes are an excellent way to supplement your available time and accumulate information or entertainment. You can learn an unlimited number of subjects, including how to speak a foreign language, speak in front of a group, be a skillful negotiator, invest in the stock market, communicate better with your mate, improve your sales skills, and how to have more time in your life. If you are really determined, you can speed listen to tapes with the use of a variable speed recorder.

◆ ***Input from VCRs:*** Use your VCR to record informational programs. You can fast-forward through the commercials. Listen to the news or an educational talk show on the television or radio. Select from thousands of CDs to play on your PC or laptop if you're traveling.

By taking advantage of the opportunities and being aware of the often invisible moments in your day, you can enhance your life almost effortlessly.

Couple time: On your life list, did you list anything that may be related to building a solid relationship with your mate? What do you need to do now to help achieve it?

"We get to be with each other more. I look forward to seeing my husband every time he walks into the room! We look for situations where we can be together at home and at work," says a survey respondent from Dothan, Alabama. This woman has an outlook! She sees her husband as an exciting element in her life, someone who lights up her life every time he walks through the door. And they have a plan: they *look* for things to do together.

◆ ***Love notes***: Couple time can be as simple as seeing each other as special and unique individuals. It only takes seconds to note something about your partner that you admire and comment on it.

As a Couple at Work, you have more opportunities than most to notice actions that occur daily and deserve some form of recognition. Try showing your sincere, verbal appreciation just once a day and see what happens.

Eye contact, a wink, a touch in passing, a shared joke, a hug in the supply room, innuendos are all ways that require little else than a conscious motion.

> "Whether people work together or not, they must
> have separate interests. Although we work
> together long hours, we still have other interests
> outside our relationship." G.B., Fayetteville, N.C.

◆　　*Personal space:* Give each other room to be alone or
take up individual interests. It is sometimes difficult to
give yourself permission to do these things. Generous
encouragement from each other will be a gift.

◆　　*Talking shop:* Whether or not you talk business at home
is up to you. Some couples have rules that no business
talk is allowed at dinner, at home or at bedtime. They
feel the need to introduce other interests and shutting
down the business at specified times helps them from
being overwhelmed and burned out. Another reason for
shutting down is realizing how children or other family
members are affected.

> "No talking about business in the bedroom.
> We're now trying to be more respectful of each
> other's time, needs, and management styles."
> C.W.N., N. Conway, NH

Others feel it is so much a part of who they are, that
talking about it anywhere and everywhere is not only
acceptable but anticipated. They say talking business
only serves to strengthen their relationship and bring
them closer together.

◆　　*Mini getaways:* Couples can do simple things like going
in late and having breakfast out on Fridays. Or they can
have a two hour lunch, massage or play a round of golf
together in the middle of the week. It usually means planning ahead, but if having couple time is important to
you, your antenna will be spanning for spontaneous
opportunities a well.

169

◆   ***Real vacations:*** The best insurance to get a vacation is to plan for it. You can prepare ahead for temporary help, training or rescheduling. Take advantage of slow seasons. Anticipation is half the fun, another reason to get it on your list of things to do. It will give you a diversion to discuss when business topics seem overwhelming.

A great way to sneak in a vacation is to tack a couple of days onto a business trip for recreation. Or attend a conference, skip the group dinner and have a romantic evening in a faraway city.

◆   ***No time for sex?*** You're not alone. In our survey, 31% of couples report their sex lives have diminished dramatically since working together. But it's not because they're not interested! The reason most of them state is not enough energy!

A gentleman from New Mexico speaks for many couples who feel no less attracted to their partners when he says it "has it's ups and downs, depending on how much pressure we are under, but still great when we find the time." Most feel the pressures of the business leave little reserve for romantic evenings.

Dr. Patricia Love and Jo Robinson in *Hot Monogamy,* say that most couples can sustain passion and intimacy for only a short time, but continue to long for the thrill and excitement they experienced when they first met.

They say as long as a couple has a mutual desire to improve their sexual lifestyle, they can create a "more sophisticated, consciously created, but even more fulfilling form of passion and intimacy."

To be a successful Couple at Work, you must be constantly communicating on many levels. You cannot assume you know what your partner wants or needs. Neither can you withhold honest sharing of your own thoughts and desires. An enhanced sexual life begins with the same tool. You must talk to each other.

> *"Both of us are often too tired/stressed-out, you know, the usual 90's stuff!"*
> *A.U., Joplin, MO*

In *Seven Weeks to Better Sex,* Domeena Renshaw, MD, addresses the issue of being too tired for sex. She describes fatigue as "your body's way of telling you that you need some rest." She says that "this simple task can accommodate both your need for rest and your need for sexual expression."

She explains that the body's first sexual sleep cycle begins ninety minutes after it goes to sleep, therefore at the end of ninety minutes, the body is at its peak sexual arousal.

She suggests on these evenings when you are too tired for sex, you set the alarm for ninety minutes, get up, take a shower and make love. The shower revives you for sex, and the sex relaxes you so you can go back to sleep.

Making a commitment to this part of your life is the same as all the other items on your To Do List. While the demands of your business may take front stage for awhile, eventually you will have to shift the balance toward your desired end result and do whatever is necessary to achieve it. Dedication, willingness and an understanding of what creates the sizzle for you and your partner is part of the equation.

We all have the same amount of time in our lives. Having the time you need to do the things you want is not about being short of it. It's about what you consider a priority and how you spend the time you have. If you work eighty hours a week to support a certain quality of lifestyle and have no time for family or friends, then you have made the lifestyle more important.

Having enough time to do what you want is a decision.

Dub

No one was more surprised than I when I said (without hesitation) an enthusiastic 'yes' to the trip. I guess I was ready to test out that notion about how good our management was.

We began rescheduling many things around the trip, but the one that counted — the biggest deal of the year with our biggest client — provided no option but to proceed one week after we left.

The yacht had been paid for, airline tickets bought, snorkeling gear packed — there was no turning back.

Taking trips without a purpose other than to relax was almost a new experience for me. It took six or eight days before I could let go and relax. But once I did, I didn't want to go back. I had set a new record for myself and I didn't even call the office until we got to the airport to fly home.

On returning, we discovered two things. One, we had a chance to step back and get a fresh view of the business and it looked good — saleable actually.

And secondly, it was as though I had jumped over some invisible hurdle by taking a real vacation and now taking time off seemed easier, almost mandatory.

And of course, time off in the Caribbean with my honey is just what our love life needed.

Janet

'You're serious?' I was shocked.

'Why not? If we haven't got the staff trained to handle things by now, we better give it up.' Was this Dub speaking?

The Caribbean: soft, clear blue and green water; warm breezes; fresh mango juice in the morning and salty margaritas at night; days and nights on a yacht rocked to sleep by ocean waves...

When we returned, brown and rested, things were purring. A complex transaction had been completed, a large profit was made, everyone was excited to show and tell how they had handled various situations. Some suggested we should be gone more often. Hmmmm — that was intriguing. The staff had done well. Very well.

We decided to give it up anyway. The vacation had reminded us why we were in the business — which was to fund our dreams and our hearts' desire. We called a business broker the next day.

More Reading About Making Time In Your Life

Bloomfield, Harold, *The Power of 5,* Rodale Press, 1994.

Covey, Stephen, *First Things First,* Simon and Schuster, 1994.

Gray, John, *Mars and Venus in the Bedroom,* HarperCollins, 1995.

Lakein, Alan, *How To Get Control of Your Time and Your Life,* The New American Library, Inc., 1974.

Levinson, Jay Conrad, *The Ninety-Minute Hour,* Dutton, 1990.

Life Insurance Marketing Research Association, *Stress ... Suffering Optional,*Managers Magazine, November 1993.

Love, Dr. Patricia & Robinson, Jo, *Hot Monogamy,* Plume/ Penguin, 1995.

Schechter, Harriet, and Gibbs, Vicki, *More Time For Sex,* Dutton, 1995.

Rechtschaffe, Stephan, *Time Shifting,* Doubleday, 1996.

Renshaw MD, Domena, *Seven Weeks to Better Sex,* Random House, 1995.

Scott, Dru, *How to Put More Time in Your Life,* Rawson, Wade Publishers, 1980.

Westheimer, Dr. Ruth, *Sex for Dummies,* IDG Books, 1995.

Survey responses *to feelings about business after being in it for awhile.*

> "It has been very satisfying, but we are reaching the point that we would like it to continue without as much time from us (we have a great staff).
> A.M.N., Jamestown, N.D.

> "After all these years, I've gone from passionate to very satisfied. It's a great job."
> Joyce Bundgaard; Denver, CO

> "We're hoping the business will grow."
> P.P., Montrose, CO

> "It's a nice business, but after 10 years I want some freedom to travel and spend winters down south." C.J., Flint, MI

Chapter 10
When It's Time To Say Goodbye

Dub

I can think of two times in my life when I was totally dedicated to a business or profession. In both cases, I reached a point where I had no more to give and no more to gain. It was time to move on.

*Also in both cases, I didn't know what I was going to do next; I just knew what I **wasn't** going to do. When I left education, I had no direction, was unaware of my abilities and knew little about my options. I just knew I had an inner hunger for change that I had to pursue, and I was scared to death.*

The second time was quite different. When Janet and I decided to sell the furniture business, I had a greater understanding of myself and my needs as a person. I knew I was an entrepreneur, that I had skills that could take me in many directions and that I enjoyed short term projects. I understood my passions and what satisfied them.

I was ready to meet my next adventure with anticipation and a

177

new confidence.

Janet

For me, selling the business was a dream come true. Although I loved the staff and enjoyed the lucrative and popular status of the recycled furniture industry, it was not my business of choice. Being tied to an office all day was too confining for my restless spirit. Now that the crisis state was over and things were running smoothly, the opportunities for creativity were no longer dramatic or varied enough to satisfy me.

Preparing for the sale was an exciting, almost surreal process. In a year and a half, Dub and I had sealed our relationship as a couple. We had new insights not only into each other but in what we could create together. The business had gone from a fledgling company to a healthy and profitable enterprise.

Our staff had become our family. We knew about their lives and they knew about ours. They were as much a part of making the company do well as we were. We partied together, planned together and even cried together.

We weren't willing to let just anybody take our spot; we cared about these people who had become so much a part of our lives. We even felt guilty about leaving them. In a short time, we had gotten into each others' hearts and it wasn't going to be easy to say goodbye.

More uncertainties loomed. Dub and I had not made any plans beyond a possible vacation and some time to figure out what we would do next. Would the business prove to be our glue?

How Do You Leave A Business?

The best way to leave a business is, of course, together. To mutually decide that it is time to move on for whatever reason — it's time, it's not working, you want to try something new, or take the money and run — is naturally the most pleasant way to end the business, the business relationship, the relationship, etc. But living in a less than perfect world, this is not always the case.

If the grim reaper decides that your partnership is over, anything you have done to prepare for the possibility will help ease the pain and burden that you face. Hopefully in your partnership agreement, you have addressed the potential of losing one partner unexpectedly and addressed a direction for the remaining partner to follow.

As is the case with most Couples at Work, the responsibilities have been divided according to the strength of skills and qualities that each partner brought to the business. Who will do these things if one of you is suddenly gone? How will you and your business be affected financially?

The emotions of your loss may blur your ability to make decisions in your best interest if you are unprepared. Calling on counsel from trusted family, friends and professionals is a good choice if you have not provided for this unhappy situation.

> *"If there are problems in the business it can spill over into the relationship. My husband has just left the business and I'm having a very hard time with his leaving."*
> *P.B., Healdsburg, CA*

Sometimes you find that you and your partner are so divided in the way you work or what you want out of life that it is no longer satisfying to work together.

When one partner wants to leave the business, what happens?

Does the business fall apart? Is the remaining partner left holding the bag, unable to cope with all the responsibilities? Is the personal relationship destroyed because one or both feel betrayed?

If you have reached the point where you want out, you have either not been able to resolve issues to your satisfaction or there are other things you need or want to do. Maybe a family member needs your attention, you want to pursue other dreams, devote more time to personal interests or health, go to school full-time, or follow another career. Whatever the reason, there are certain things you can do to make the exit go smoothly.

When To Quit

Quitting can be selling, bequeathing, hiring managers, filing bankruptcy, or simply dissolving the company and dispersing the assets. It is removing yourself from the daily operation and/or financial responsibility of the business.

If quitting has not been included in your long-term game plan, you may be caught off guard if you are suddenly faced with the symptoms of dissatisfaction with your business. Among the warning signs are unceasing boredom, health problems, constant and long-term financial difficulties, exhaustion, staff and customer tension, destructive and unresolved conflict, or frustration and family disintegration.

If you do not act on these warning signals you may make serious trade-offs in your relationships, mental and physical health, financial security, and lifelong enrichment.

As a Couple at Work, it is important to regularly review your life goals, why you started your business, why you are working together, and what you hope for the future. If your business or your business relationship as a couple no longer serves your pursuits, you may be faced with some tough decisions. If it is unlikely to change, it may be time to consider separating your-selves from the business or as business partners.

When One Of You Goes

Unless a couple has planned for the departure of one partner, this can be one of the most painful and disagreeable of partings. If tension is high and respect is low between two people, harsh words can undermine the relationship, business, morale, cus-tomer rapport, and staff loyalty.

> *"When you own a business that represents all your joint assets you must resolve the problems."*
> Robert LeGresley, Lawrence, KS

Since you have a lot to gain by working it out, you may want to take a few steps to try and salvage the situation.

♦ **_Identify the source:_** Why are you unhappy? Is it the work or the product? Do you feel unable to work with each other? Why? Be specific about what circumstances make you feel this way. Is your life out of balance?

♦ **_Consider options:_** Could job responsibilities be rear-ranged? Could you change roles from time to time? If your life is out of balance how could you regain con-trol? Do you need to learn how to communicate with each other?

♦ **_Talk, talk, talk:_** And listen, listen, listen. Although exhausting at times, eventually the truth will emerge and you will have something concrete to work with.

♦ **_Involve a mediator:_** If you can't communicate with each other rationally, involve a third person. Family business counselors, private counselors, coaches, and professional mediators can help you see more clearly what is going on and help you reach a fair and objective solution.

If you are unable to find an agreeable solution and you do not have a partnership agreement to guide you, here are some things to keep in mind as you proceed through the division.

◆   *Act professionally:* If you can't keep business and personal feelings apart, get help from a business or private counselor. You do not want to lose business or alienate customers and employees.

◆   *Acknowledge positive contributions made by your partner:* Just because you no longer want to work together does not mean that your partner is worthless. Some couples are acutely aware of their partners' input and choose to dissolve their personal relationship and continue working together.

◆   *Keep your issues private:* Your business and often your financial well-being may depend on your ability to maintain a harmonious front to employees and clients. This does not mean keeping secrets. Employees and customers need to know about transitions and they especially need to be reassured that their security or position is not threatened. Change is often unsettling.

◆   *Involve a third person:* If you are unable to be civil to one another, enlist a third person to help with communication until you can resolve your personal conflicts.

If You Plan To Sell It

For some Couples at Work, the chaos and activity of business start-up and development provide the thrill of entrepreneurship. Once things are running smoothly and boredom sets in, a lack of enthusiasm and creativity can reverse some of the early successes. At these times, couples can become their own worst enemies. By selling the business when it is young, they can maintain their excitement and ingenuity in new enterprises.

In other situations, couples have discovered a lucrative business in an industry that is not particularly appealing, but see a temporary commitment as an opportunity to fund other ventures or interests.

For couples who have no family available or interested in carrying on the business, selling can provide retirement income.

> *"The business is not as creative as it was getting started and building it up. Now we need a new creative challenge and some down time."*
> A.L., Paducah, KY

If you recognize yourselves as start-up addicts, opportunity seekers or retirement-directed, the earlier you prepare for departure, the better. As soon as possible — the day you open — begin making your business saleable. The idea is to offer an attractive company with a solid foundation that will be profitable and manageable.

In *Cashing In, Getting the Most When You Sell Your Business,* authored by Berger, Berger and Eastwood, four essential areas are targeted for the seller to spruce up for potential buyers. Included are structure, business activity, employees, personnel, and finances. A detailed assessment checklist is included in their book.

Whatever advice you take, you cannot go wrong if you heed the following guidelines. They apply whether you are selling your business, trying to get additional funding or seeking new partners.

◆ ***Organize legally:*** Whatever form of business structure you choose, sole proprietorship, partnership, corporation, etc., form it legally and meet all the requirements to maintain its integrity.

◆ ***Develop a business plan:*** Include the history of your product, the market share you maintain, what the competitors control, your marketing strategy, the future prognosis of sales and how you will counter outside factors that may influence your business.

◆ ***Show growth:*** Growth needs to be steadily increasing; some months may show decreased activity, especially if your business is seasonal; if the overall trend is upward, your business looks healthy.

◆ ***Keep records on everything:*** Track inventory, performance of employees, results of advertising, correspondence with anyone, income and expenses, phone calls, conversations, etc. You will be amazed at the resource provided by detailed record keeping when trying to reconstruct events.

◆ ***Have trained employees:*** Personnel is one of the most challenging components of any business. The less a buyer has to worry about this arena at the start, the better. Put lots of energy into cultivating stable, well-informed and happy employees. Keep performance plans, evaluations and salary schedules with employees updated and applicable.

◆ ***Develop manuals:*** Describe in detail every task required to run your business. List step-by-step instructions for how each should be performed. Write job descriptions for every employee.

◆   ***Spruce up:*** Acquire a polished look from the start. Create an environment that reflects the type of business you have. Be organized and clean. Work hard to make it look easy and automatic.

◆   ***Get help:*** When it is time to sell your business, call in your accountant, attorney, business broker or someone who is an expert in selling a business. There are many factors to consider and many creative ways to structure a sale. Unless you work full-time at these details, you may cheat yourself out of the most equitable and profitable approach.

Couples who pay attention to how they look are more likely to wink and nod at each other and squeeze hands under the table when their business activities and records are exposed to a buyer's scrutiny.

When You Plan To Pass It On

If you are a Couple at Work that hopes to hand the baton to your children or other family members and you plan to do it well, you have committed to a process much larger than passing over the company checkbook and operations.

Before expecting your offspring or relatives to assume control of your company you will want to be open and honest in allowing them to try on the shoes and then make their own decisions about what is best for them.

◆   ***Make sure they have the desire:*** If working in your business is not their hearts' desire, something will be sacrificed if they do it anyway. It may be their happiness, their creative spirit or it may be the business you have worked so hard to build. It could be all these things. Whatever it is, it is probably not worth it.

◆　***Make sure they are qualified:*** Not everybody is cut out to be an entrepreneur, nor does everyone want to manage the many facets of a business, supervise employees or prospect for clients. To place someone who is low key and artistic, with no interest in business, in a demanding management position is unfair and unproductive.

◆　***Encourage experience outside your business:*** Those who have worked for different companies have a broader perspective of the outside world. They have a better chance of making the right decision about whether or not to carry on your business or chart territory that is more appealing to them. Their exposure from other jobs may bring valuable experience if they do decide to join you.

◆　***Provide adequate training and education:*** For anyone to take over your business they must have a broad understanding of what it is about. Take them to meetings, include them in discussions about all types of issues and ask them for input.

Let them make mistakes. See that they have a mentor or someone trustworthy to show them the ropes and teach them the details. If schooling will help them be more successful or confident, assure that they get it.

◆　***Make plans for yourself:*** Leaving a business is like having your children leave home. Empty spots show up in your heart and your head. The swiftness with which you are replaced and the loyalties are shifted can be shocking.

> " We are looking forward to the next adventure together."   T.O., Monterey, CA

Expect it and prepare for it. Know what you are going to do with your life A.B. (After Business). If you are anything like the many couples in our survey, you will already be planning your next venture together. And if you've been applying good time management, you know where you're going and the speed bumps won't be near as intimidating.

Shed A Few Tears

Regardless of the circumstances, letting go of a business that you have created, grown and harvested is rarely an easy experience. But it is easier if you plan for it and prepare yourself emotionally, financially and physically.

No matter how you feel about the business, there is a part of you that will always be invested in its existence. What happens to it in the future will probably always be of some curiosity to you. You did it together, you made it happen. It is a product of your union, your strengths, your determination, and your perseverance. It is your legacy and the memories are yours forever.

Dub

'Parting is such sweet sorrow.' The staff had become a big part of our lives. In leaving, I first felt that we were abandoning them. But in less time than it took us to pack our things, they got over it and we did too.

Launching the company, creating its growth and watching it take on a personality of its own was only part of the reward. For me, it represented my personal evolution as a sound businessman, something that had been important to me for a long time.

As we walked away, I breathed in the freedom of accomplishment. For the first time in my life, I felt a release from my own expectations. I gave myself permission to do what I wanted, to follow my true passion for the first time in my life.

Janet

The sale went well. As if by magic, the right buyer appeared. We stayed on for a short period to assist with the transition and were on our own by the holidays — exactly a year and a half from the date of my original commitment.

We were standing on the edge of everything we'd ever wanted — togetherness, freedom, funding and choices. The future became our prize — a vast unknown beckoning us to jump in and experience the promise. We got married, took a year off to travel and regroup, settled in Denver and began our journey into forever.

More Reading About Leaving A Business

Baechler, Mary, *Death of a Marriage,* Inc., April 1994.

Berger, Lisa and Donelson and Eastwood, C. William, *Cashing In, Getting the Most When You Sell Your Business,* Warner Books, 1988.

Boman, Jerry and Joanne, *Sustaining a Business — After a Divorce,* Nation's Business, 1994.

Karofsky, Paul I., *When 'For Better or For Worse' Becomes Worse...,* Northeastern University's Center for Family Business, March 1996.

Nelton, Sharon, *The Agony of Quitting a Family Firm,* Nation's Business, October 1995.

Singer, Merv and Hine, Harrison W., *The Price of 'Protecting' Your Family,* Nation's Business, September 1995.

Vinton, Lisa L. and Tow, Stephen, *A Marriage — and a Business — In Crisis,* Nation's Business, July 1995.

Survey responses *to the question "If your business partnership ended, what would happen to your relationship or your business?"*

> *"It would not end because we jointly agreed to sell the business — we would then create another joint business."*
> *A.J., Ada, Oklahoma*

> *"I am concerned that not working together may cause a break-up. Only the future will tell."* *P.B., Healdsburg, CA*

> *"We have the business up for sale. There is not enough money to cover the bills. We can't take the pressure anymore."*
> *B.C., Little Rock, AK*

Chapter 11
Family Matters

Dub

Until the summer of 1992, I really had not spent enough time around my daughter, who was now 25 years old, to know her skills, her dreams or what she expected of me and our relationship.

That summer, the year before Janet came to work with me, Amy came to work in the business. Although it didn't start out well, it turned out to be the beginning of a new era in our relationship.

When Amy arrived, I had the attitude that she was part of me and what I represented. I expected her to have my work ethic, want to work my hours, have my drive and do more work with better quality than any other employee.

The first week was hell. She was one disappointment after another. I was constantly upset and yelling at her. During the second week, things took a turn when I assigned her a job on the computer that I hated and basically couldn't do. She was great. She took charge of the new software programs and I began taking orders from her to help accomplish tasks.

By the end of the summer, I had a new respect for her. On a day in and day out basis in a work environment, we were exposed to aspects of each other that we didn't even think about in our traditional roles as father and daughter.

Janet

Although Dub and I did not work together with our children in the furniture business, we did have some independent experiences with them on other occasions. When my son Greg was 10 years old, we lived in the mountains on the summit above Lake Tahoe, California in the tiny community of Little Norway.

Living in a remote wilderness area did not provide the usual after-school jobs of newspaper routes or lawn mowing. So to raise a little spending money, every day after school Greg carried his air popper up to a little resort restaurant and sold popcorn for 25 cents a bag (you can do this kind of thing in mountain communities).

Being a resort area, the tourist season was based on skiing so business was slow for much of the year. If he collected 50 cents on any one night he had done well. To make matters worse, he was soon faced with competition when the restaurant owner's son became intrigued with the idea. Being in a privileged position, he got permission to set up his 'popcorn business' in a better location.

Greg soon tired of the futility of his venture. His profits were used up buying popcorn, butter and bags. Too much of his time was spent cleaning the air popper, walking up and down the hill to the resort and sitting around hoping for a customer.

I had two distinct reactions. The first was disappointment that

*his efforts hadn't paid off in more sales. I wanted him to experi-
ence the thrill of being in business; of creating something and
getting rewarded for it.*

*The second reaction was more important. In the process, I
discovered a side of him that I hadn't seen before. He had taken
his business seriously and when he quit it wasn't because of
childish impatience or lack of determination. He had evaluated
his position in a businesslike fashion. I discovered he was analytical — he compared his expenses against his profits, factored
in his time and weighed it against his personal needs; he was
creative — he positioned himself in the restaurant to get the
most visibility and made a big sign to draw attention to himself;
he was prudent — he knew when to quit.*

*Could it be that children have qualities that go unnoticed
until we see them at work?*

Children Are Unique

Couples at Work who work with their children have either
found buried treasure or opened Pandoras Box. In our survey,
couples report they were proud to discover their children were
"so personable," had "leadership and dependability traits," were
"so competent," had "strong sales skills," and "good logical
thinking."

Others were disappointed to find that their offspring were
"not interested in business," "strong-willed and angry," or a
"poor worker." Although there are many factors contributing to
what position your children have, the message that it can go
either way is real. Your children have their own personalities,
dreams and desires and may or may not embrace your business.
Your job is to accept that and plan accordingly.

Involving children in a couple-owned business is sometimes

193

a given, particularly if the business is home-based and often difficult to separate family from business. Some Couples at Work make a decision not to bring their children on board feeling that it would be too stressful trying to switch back and forth from parent to employer.

Whatever you decide, there are things to consider both for and against.

Advantages Of Working With Your Children

If your children work with you, there are many opportunities present to enhance your relationship.

> *"My goal was to have my family work together and be together more."*
> Kathy Larson, Sandy, UT

♦ **You spend more time together:** Couples at Work often spend long hours doing business. Most couples that work together say that what they like best is being together so much. There is no disconnect as each goes off to another environment. By including your children, they too can reap the subtle rewards of just being next to you.

♦ **They are more a part of your life:** What you do during the day is not a mystery. They see what you do, how you do it and even help you with it. They have a better understanding of you and you of them.

♦ **They get work experience:** It's tough to get that first job. Depending on what they do and how long they do it, they have the opportunity to be well equipped to find employment outside your business.

> *"Child care is so difficult for young couples today. It's expensive and often dangerous to leave children with sitters, schools or nannies. Working together — there is so much more understanding of children's needs. When I worked for a large company, my boss was not at all compassionate about my child care needs. Working together enhanced our marriage as well as our family."* Karen Weiss, Tamarac, FL

◆ ***You know where they are:*** The worry of child care when they are young, or mischief when they are older, can be a source of constant anxiety. If you find ways to include them in your business, you have a better chance of influencing their activities.

◆ ***They learn business skills:*** Being around a business is exposure to another world. Whether they are sweeping the floor, answering the phone, doing research on the Internet, or managing another division, they are automatically absorbing the elements of the work place.

◆ ***You learn new things about them:*** Most of us, including children, have one set of characteristics that we use in private and another in public. A business environment often stimulates inactive qualities and provides a catalyst for their development.

◆ ***They learn new things about you:*** Instead of seeing you only as a caretaker, they may see you as an individual. Seeing you at work using skills that produce results or respect from people outside your family can be an enlightening experience for children.

◆ ***They learn about themselves:*** While going off to work may seem ideal and romantic to a child who is required to pack off to school everyday, actual work experience brings dreams down to a more realistic perspective. They may also find that they have a talent for talking to customers, handling many things at once or enjoy pressure. They may discover that your business does not interest them at all and decide to pursue another career.

Disadvantages Of Working With Your Children

◆   ***They are in an awkward position:*** They are caught between parents and employees. It is difficult, if not impossible to separate the parent-child relationship. Because you are the parent, they may feel constantly under scrutiny both from you and others. If they make a mistake, it may be magnified and if they do well it may be downplayed.

◆   ***You are in an awkward position:*** It is natural to want your children to do well, to make you proud. If you have employees they may be overly sensitive if you react favorably to your child's accomplishments, feeling that you are playing favorites. If you are frugal with your compliments, your child may feel unappreciated. If your child's performance is undesirable or if he makes a mistake, you may feel embarrassed or responsible.

> *"Our 19 year-old thought we expected too much of her because she was family."*
> *D.A., Stanford, CT*

◆   ***You expect more of them:*** Because parents feel accountable for their children and are anxious to have them behave in ways that reflect good upbringing, it is easy to demand that they accomplish more than others, and do so with better than excellent standards.

> *"Our children resent our time with the business.*
> *They want us with them more."*
> R. S., Lee's Summit, MO

♦ ***They feel deprived of "regular" life:*** Couples at Work can easily become obsessed with their business. They may talk about it on the way home, at dinner, after dinner, on weekends, at breakfast, and even on family vacations or outings. Children living in this environment resent the incessant chatter about business and long for the family who places its focus on the children and other interests.

♦ ***They are treated like children instead of employees:*** Leaving the relationship of parent-child behind and all the interactions that go with it can be challenging. If children are told what to do when other employees are invited to participate in a discussion about a topic, it is demeaning. They may foster contempt or resentment if they are given constant direction when others are allowed to be independent.

♦ ***They may act like children instead of employees:*** It can be embarrassing and distracting if your children have temper tantrums, expect you to feed them and give them spending money before payday. If they interrupt or confront you in inappropriate ways your days will be filled with unacceptable complications.

♦ ***They may hate the business:*** There are no guarantees that they will love your business, which can be disappointing if not devastating. If you get them involved while they are young, you will both have plenty of time to pursue other alternatives.

When They Work With You

Once your children arrive in the workplace, the dynamics of what they will do, how they will fit in and how your relationship will change will become a precedent. If you have other employees they may be uneasy about how your children's presence will affect them. Confronting as many issues as you can from the beginning will ease the transition.

♦ *Prepare your children:* Before they begin working with you, talk to them about what you expect from them and what they can expect from you. Teach them how work behavior is different from family behavior.

♦ *Prepare your employees:* Let them know when your children will begin work and what they will be doing. Assure them that their jobs are secure.

♦ *Give your children a specific job with specific duties:* By giving them exact performance requirements they will have a sense of purpose and contribution. A specific job may be running errands, necessary cleaning or managing the sales force. You do not want them standing or fooling around because they aren't sure what they are supposed to be doing. Neither do you want them to develop a negative appreciation for work.

♦ *Train them:* No matter how small or prestigious a job is, children need to be taught the same as anyone else. Send them to school or workshops if necessary, give them an in-house mentor, or do it yourself, but help them succeed by giving them the appropriate training.

♦ *Treat them like any other employee:* Give them job descriptions, make them accountable for their work, praise and reward them, evaluate their performance, and pay them what the job is worth.

> "We became friends and not the enemy."
> DU. Baton Rouge, LA

- ◆ **Respect them:** Don't forget that they have opinions, desires, and feelings just like you. Correct them in private. Assume they are capable of learning, having productive ideas and fulfilling their job requirements if you give them the tools needed.

What If It Just Doesn't Work?

Family members may inherit many common characteristics; they may look like you, talk like you, gesture like you, and even have the same interests. Then again, they may not!

If your children don't show the interest in your venture that you'd hoped for, or aren't performing the way you expected, you can explore some ideas before giving up on them. Make sure it is lack of interest and not a lack of something else.

- ◆ Do they have enough time for their friends and other interests?

- ◆ Have they been properly trained?

- ◆ Is their relationship with you nurturing, loving and supportive?

- ◆ Is their relationship with other employees comfortable?

- ◆ Are they able to get to the job site without unnecessary hassle?

- ◆ Do they feel adequate, competent and appreciated?

◆ Would working somewhere else give them more exposure and possibly more appreciation for the situation they have with you?

Keep in mind that children are not always able to express their frustration. If they do not admit to any problems, act on your hunches and try, within reason, to make differences for them.

> *"Our kids have always been free to be or not be a part of the business."* E.N., Limon, CO

Don't take it personally if they simply do not like your business. Your goal as a parent is to help your children grow into independent, contributing adults. If you are teaching them to have a To Do List for life, they probably have at least one item having something to do with feeling fulfilled. If they are artists, clothing designers or poets and your business manufactures computer chips, sells real estate or counsels small business, they are *obligated* to decline your offer.

Dub

What I learned with Amy is that your children need to be as qualified for the job you give them as anyone else. I had not treated her as I did other employees. I would never hire a computer person to do warehouse work. She had been assigned menial tasks that were physically impossible for her and that frustrated her.

Amy caught on faster than I did about doing what she wanted with her life. I followed in my father's footsteps in the field of education and Amy followed me. It was expected and it was assumed. It took me twelve years to get out of education and another nineteen to find and follow my passion.

Amy lasted three years in education, had no interest in the furniture business and is now in San Francisco working in software.

I wouldn't have it any other way.

Janet

Since Greg has grown up, he has became a computer whiz. Now when he helps me out (mostly from the goodness of his heart) he does so with such diligence and perseverance that again I see a side of him that went unnoticed when I relate to him as my son. I see that he is a problem solver, challenged by the difficult and determined to find solutions.

We have no plans to work together in business. He is following his interest in computer science while Dub and I trek off into the sunset following our dreams. But who knows? Maybe someday we'll need his computer skills in some more permanent way. Or maybe, just maybe...he'll hire us!

More Reading About Working With Your Family

McMenamin, Brigid, *Family Matters,* Forbes, September 1993.

Estess, Patricia Schiff, *Parent Trap,* Entrepreneur, Oct 1994.

Frishkoff, Patricia and Kaye, Kenneth, *Case Study: When a Holiday is No Fun,* Nation's Business, December 1995.

Spragins, *Employees as Family,* Inc., December 1992.

Fenn, Donna, *Are Your Kids Good Enough to Run Your Business?* Inc., August 1994.

Survey responses *to what it's like to work with your children.*

"We have a really close accepting relationship with our children. There were tough times, but we always encouraged them to follow their own hearts." E.N., Durham, N.C.

"The children blossomed as they worked with us." Jane F. Edwards, Edenton, N.C.

"It was good for our son who was very quiet and 'came out' while working in the retail store." Robert A. LeGresley, Lawrence, KS

I discovered they interact well with people." Doug Larson, Sandy, UT

"They have great respect for us and their work habits show that respect." Donna Marriott "They are strong, responsive workers." Robert Marriot, St. Augustine, FL

Chapter 12
Master Minding

Janet and Dub

It just wouldn't be fair to take all the credit for the success we had so quickly in our business together without sharing a technique that helped us be clear about our goals, focus on our direction and take action to make it all happen. In a year and a half the business had become profitable and saleable enough to fund our dreams for the future. We had taken it from a question mark to a pronounced exclamation point. We had done it because we complimented each other so well, because our lessons came fast and we listened, and because we were determined and well — obsessed.

But there was an element that we are certain was by far the most important ingredient of all.

Over the years, we have, both independently and together, studied many philosophies for successful living such as visualization, meditation, positive thinking, mind over matter, and more. We are convinced that there are sources much bigger than our own physical presence to help us understand the difficulties of life and steer us toward fulfillment and peace.

Janet

In the year prior to working with Dub, I had been meeting once a week with a friend to meditate on our lives and focus on the qualities we hoped to develop to be more loving and contributing human beings. The results we experienced were overwhelming. Our lives changed in remarkable ways — we did not become rich and famous. We became more accepting and forgiving of life in general but we also began to take actions that we had feared, at least subconsciously, in the past.

Dub

I have always been open and eager to explore ways that will better my life, and I was anxious to incorporate the method that Janet had been doing into our new life together. So we began, once a week, taking thirty to forty minutes to focus on how we could improve the various elements of our daily life.

Dub and Janet

Because we were entwined on so many levels, we expanded the process and the benefits we experienced were inspirational.

We called it Master Minding and here's what we did.

Master Mind Your Way To Success

Master Minding is not something we thought up nor is it new. In 1953, a book written by Napoleon Hill called *How to Raise Your Own Salary,* describes the process of Master Minding through an interview with Andrew Carnegie. Mr. Carnegie, who succeeded in raising himself from a laborer to the greatest industrialist ever, offered the world's first practical philosophy of success based on his own lifetime experiences.

He says that Master Minding is not a man-made principle, but rather a part of natural law. He says we may not be able to influence this law but we "can understand it and adapt ourselves to it in ways that will bring us great benefits, no matter who we are or what our calling may be."

The process described by Mr. Carnegie involves gathering a group of trusted experts with specific qualities from many fields to meet with the purpose of supporting and strengthening a particular objective.

While our intent was the same, we adapted the process to include just two people and we concentrated our energy on very specific outcomes. Our basis was believing the premise of this book, that when two people join together in an honest attempt to create something for the good of both, a third and more powerful effect is created.

◆ ***Set aside a definite time:*** Find a time that works with your lifestyle. We experimented first with Sunday nights, thinking it would give us a good beginning for the week. But Sunday was our only day with no business commitments, so we changed it to Monday nights around eight o'clock. It turned out to be a good choice because we were back in the swing of things and more conscious of what we wanted to create.

◆ ***Set the scene:*** Turn off the answering machine, unplug the phone or close the door. Find a spot where interruptions are unlikely. Wear unrestrictive clothes, get a blanket if you might get cold or open a window if it's too hot. Don't get too comfortable; you don't want to fall asleep! We had two high back chairs that we placed on either side of an end table in an undisturbed location. We turned out the lights and lit candles.

◆ ***Review your thoughts:*** Have a short conversation about things on your mind that you would like to change, improve or influence in some way. Make sure you each have a few minutes to express the things that are foremost in your thoughts. You do not need to say everything you are thinking, just address the most important issues. The rest will automatically come up as you get into the process.

◆ ***Meditate for twenty minutes:*** The purpose of meditating is to clear your mind from all the "junk thoughts" you collect everyday so you can hear your inner thoughts. By listening to music and not allowing any thoughts to overtake your mind you will still yourself.

If you are not used to meditating, lots of busy thoughts will try to get in; just brush them away and concentrate on the music. Listen to every note and instrument, imagine the musicians and feel the music.

Choose music that does not have any associations for you. You do not want to start thinking about someone from your past or feeling emotions that may interfere with your current purpose. We made our own tape, picking out pieces from various artists that were neutral but relaxing to both of us.

◆ ***Sit for a few minutes:*** When the music has finished, allow whatever thoughts arise; sometimes you will have a new insight on a situation. Imagine the issues you talked about before you meditated with new outcomes.

◆ ***Verbalize the things on your mind:*** Take turns speaking aloud. State how you wish a situation to be as though it has already happened. If you are in the process of finding a new bookkeeper, say "I see an honest and trustworthy bookkeeper sitting behind the desk. She is keeping the records up-to-date, processing payroll in an accurate and timely manner and building good rapport with everyone." Your intent must be for the good of all or it doesn't work.

We tried to not only say what we wanted, but *believed* that we could create it.

◆   ***Repeat back what you heard:*** Immediately after your partner has verbalized aloud, repeat back what you heard. Say it as though you see it has occurred. This act makes you listen, support and invest in your partners' desires. It also gives you a very privileged insight into your partner. This is a very powerful step.

Don't worry about remembering everything your partner says. Anything you remember and repeat are valuable.

Master Minding works. It helps you see exactly what you are striving for or what bothers you instead of functioning with a dull awareness that something isn't quite right. If you are sincere in your desire to improve your life, business, relationships, and overall contribution to society, this technique will help you get there. It's a simple process and takes very little time.

As a Couple at Work you have more reason than ever to use this dynamic means for creating the life you want. It worked for Andrew Carnegie. It worked for Napoleon Hill. It worked for us.

It can work for you too.

More Reading About Building Success

Covey, Stephen R. *The 7 Habits of Highly Effective People,* Simon and Schuster, 1990.

Hill, Napoleon, *Grow Rich With Peace of Mind*, Fawcett Publications, 1967, and *How to Raise Your Own Salary,* Napoleon Hill Associates, 1953.

Schwartz, Ph.D., David J., *The Magic of Thinking Big,* Simon and Schuster, 1980.

Index

A

A Little Book of Forgiveness 142
Aburdene, Patricia 79
  Megatrends 2000, 79
Active 110
Advantages
  appreciation 21
  balance 21
  bonds 21
  common goals 21
  confidence 21
  exercise 20
  explain 20
  hug 20
  kiss 20
  rearrange 20
  Share 21
  strength 21
  team effort 21
  trustworthy 21
  worry 20
Agreement 33
  Partnership 33
Altlernatives 27
  dreams 29
  family member 28
  goal 28
  hire 28
  home 28
  option 28
  part time 28
  partner 28
  student 28
  temporary 28
American Couples 87
  Blumstein and Schwartz 87

Andrew Carnegie 206, 209
Aspirations 91
  business 91
Assess 96
  desire 96
  interpretation 97
  money style 96
  past 97
Attitude
  71, 74, 76, 90, 91, 95
  money 91
Authority 77

B

Balance
  90, 159, 161, 165, 181
Barnett, Frank and Sharan 20
  Working Together 20
Being together 22, 160, 194
Berger, Berger and Eastwood
  183
  *Cashing In; Getting The
    Most When You Sell Your
    Business*
Blumstein and Schwartz 87
  American Couples 87
Boss 55
  appearance 60
  best 58
  boss 57, 59, 60, 61, 70
  business 58
  comfort 58
  customers 57
  employees 57
  equal posts 59
  expertise 58
  flexibility 58
  personalities 59
  productive 58
  title 57
  traditional 58

united front 58
Business 178
  leave 178
  pass it on 185
  passing it on 185
  prepare 183
  saleable 183
  selling 182
Business structure 46
  accounting 47
  buying 47
  clerical 47
  customer service 47
  maintenance 47
  operations 47
  personnel 47
  purchasing: 47
  sales & marketing 46

C

*Cashing In, Getting the Most
  When You Sell Your
  Business*
  Berger, Berger and
    Eastwood 183
Characteristics 21
  invisible 21
  special 21
Children 193
  at work 193
  awkward 196
  business skills 195
  duties 198
  employees
    196, 197, 198, 199
  expectations 196
  experience 194
  part of 194
  prepare 198
  regular life 197
  respect 199

  together 194
  whereabouts 195
Clientele 92
Clifford and Warren 35
  Partnership Book 35
Communicator 109
Compensation 92, 144
Complimentary qualities 46
Confidence 73, 74, 109, 162
  achievements 74
  capture 73
  control 74
  history 74
  informed 73, 74
  insurance 73
  relationships 74
  self 74
  sense of humor 74
  women 73
Confident 109
Conflict
  association 136
  heart connection 136
  help 144
  positive force 138
  resolution 138
  techniques 139
Confronter 87
Conversation
  men 75
  women 75
Conversation. 75
  connection 75
  men 75
  women 75
Covey, Stephen 138
  *The 7 Habits of Highly
    Effective People* 138
Creative 108
Cultural differences 95D
Deborah Tannen 75
  You Just Don't Understand,

75
Defensive 72, 74, 144
Descriptors 111
Desire
    assessing 24
    conflict resolution 96
    understanding 24
Determined 108
Disadvantages
    income 23
    independent 22
    personal differences 22
    stifled 22
    unattractive 22
    yin and yang 23
Divide 43
    business structure 46
Doer 113
Duties 45, 46, 48, 77, 198
    assessing 48
    dividing 46
    education 48
    personality 47
    priorities 49
    strengths 46
    suitability 47
    survey 45
    weaknesses 46

E

Education
    48, 50, 124, 177, 186, 200
Employees 197, 198

F

Family 185
    children 193
    desire 185
    education 186
    experience 186

matters 191
other jobs 186
passing it on 185
qualified 185
survey 193
Family business
    50, 92, 124, 144, 181
Family Centers 50
Family life 27, 39
Feeler 111
Follower 110
Forgive 142
Fulfillment 48

G

Genders 60, 121
Gibb, Vicki T. 160
    No Time For Sex
Goals
    94, 99, 108, 110, 155, 159, 180
Good-humor woman 71
    attitude
        71, 74, 76, 90, 91, 95
Goodbye 177
    business 178
    family 185
    mediator 181
    one goes 181
    pass 185
    passing it on 185
    plans 186
    quit 180
    selling 182
    tears 187
Growth 92
Guide to Marriage & Money
    95 Johansen and Brown

H

Heart connection 136
Hoarder 87

How to Raise Your Own Salary
     206
   Napoleon Hill 206
Humor 72, 73, 74, 109
   male, female 71
   well-intended 72

I

Independent 108
Intimacy 40, 75, 134
Invisible 67
   woman 67
Issues 38
   equal 39, 69

J

Johansen and Brown
   Guide to Marriage & Money
     95
Jung, Carl 111

L

Ladies 70
   lighten 70
Leader 109
Leave 178
   business 178
   mediator 181
   one goes 181
   quit 180
LeDoux, Dr. Wendy 98
   Money and Marriage 98
Lighten 70

M

Mackoff, Dr. Barbara 70
   What Mona Lisa Knew 70
Maintenance 160
Management
   best 115

differences 114
feeler 111
individual 107
personality
     107, 111, 113, 115
styles 107
survey 107
Management styles
     23, 107, 115, 123
   opposition 23
Manager 110
Master Minding 205
   Andrew Carnegie 206
   meditate 208
   Napoleon Hill 206
   process 206
McAllen, Jack 70
   The Boss Should Be as a
     Woman 70
Mediator 181
Meditate 208
Megatrends 2000, 79
   Aburdene, Patricia 79
   Naisbitt, John 79
Mellan, Olivia 95
   Money Harmony 95
Men 72, 75
   announce 78
   asking for opinions 76
   benefit 75
   core driver 75
   creativity 88
   credit 78
   frustrated 77
   humor 71
   hunters, gatherers 96
   kid around 72
   kidding around 72
   money 87
   negotiations 75
   one-upmanship 75

respect 77
training 78
unlimited thinking 88
vision 90
visualization 88
ways to support 77
Money 85
 budget 94
 clientele 92
 compensation 92
 conflicts 95
 cultural differences 95
 disagreements 87
 goal 94
 growth 92
 Guide to Marriage & Money
  95
 habits 87
 how spent 87
 joint responsibility 99
 management 87
 men 87
 Money Harmony 95
 perceptions 98
 philosophy 93
 priorities 87
 problem 95
 product/service 93
 profits 94
 purpose 91
 survey 95
 tactics 95
 viewpoints 87
 women 87
Money and Marriage 98
 LeDoux, Dr. Wendy 98
Money Harmony 95
 Olivia Mellan 95
More Time for Sex 160
 Gibbs, Vicki T. 160
 Schechter, Harriet 160

N

Naisbitt, John 79
 Megatrends 2000, 79
Napoleon Hill 206, 209
 *How to Raise Your Own
  Salary* 206

O

Opposing
 attitudes 90
 styles 107
Organized 110
Organizing 163
Outsource 50

P

Partnership Agreement
  36, 38, 45, 179, 182
 children 39
 compensation 39
 disputes 38
 distribution 38
 duties 38
 ending 38
 family and friends 39
 funded 38
 goals 38
 items addressed 38
 personal chores 39
 profits 39
 sale 38
 social life 39
 term 38
 time 39
 type of business 38
 value 38
 withdrawals 38
Partnership Book 35
 Clifford and Warren
Pension 93

Personality
  communicator 109
  confident 109
  creative 108
  descriptors 111
  determined 108
  doer 113
  feeler 111, 112
  follower 110
  independent 108
  intuitor 112
  leader 109
  manager 110
  organized 110
  planner 110
  reliant 108
  reserved 109
  restless 108
  risk-taker 108
  security conscious 109
  self-disciplined 108
  spontaneous 111
  subordinate 110
  tentative 109
  thinker 112
  understanding 47
  unique 47
Personality traits
    47, 113, 115
Perspective 71
Philosophy 161, 206
Planner 110
Popcorn, Faith 80
  The Popcorn Report 80
Priorities 49, 87
  anecdote 49
  avoidance 49
  communication 49
  complex 49
  dealing with 49
  disagreements 87
  inadequate 49

  misinterpreted 49
  perception 49
  simple 49
  unqualified 49
Purpose 91

Q

Qualified
    26, 49, 50, 185, 200
  skills 117

R

Relationship 18
Reliant 108
Reserved 109
Restless 108
Risk-taker 108
Round table 91
Rules 121
  temporary 121

S

Safety 90
Salaries 95
Schechter 160
Schechter, Harriet 160
  No Time For Sex
Seasonal planning: 162
Security conscious 109
Security-conscious 87
Self confident 70
Self-Confidence 74
Self-disciplined 108
Selling 182
  business plan 184
  employees 184
  growth 184
  manuals 184
  organize legally 183
  records 184

spruce up 183
Sense of humor 70, 73, 74
  attitude 71
  laughable 71
  male, female 71
  perfect 71
  perspective 71
  women 70
Society 69, 76, 96, 121, 209
  men 69
  transitional 76
Soul connection
  conflict 137
Soul searching 27
Spendthrift 87
Spontaneous 111
Squanderer 87
Stephen Covey
  The 7 Habits of Highly
    Effective People 138
Style 96
  assess 96
  money 96
Subordinate 110
Success
  free 89
  fulfilled 89
  proud 89
  women 89T
Taboo 71
  women 71
Talk 74
  business 89
  interpret 75
  men 74
  misunderstood 75
  negotiations 75
  women 75
Tears 187
Techniques 139, 142
Tentative 109
The 7 Habits of Highly

Effective People 138
  Covey. Stephen 138
The Boss Should Be as a
  Woman 70
  Jack McAllen 70
The Eight Essential Steps to
  Conflict Resolution 140
The Popcorn Report 80
  Faith Popcorn 80
Third brain 19
  wegos 20,78
Time
  business 161
  couple time 168
  delegation 161
  family 165
  getting 159
  household 164
  life list 159
  maintenance 160
  mentality 157
  organizing 163
  prioritizing 162
  seasonal planning: 162
  self development 167
  special projects 160
  to do list 154
Time off
  20, 151, 153, 158, 159, 173
Title 60, 61
  image 61
  marketing device 61
  non traditional 61
  playful 61
  public purpose 60
  thoughts about 60
  tool 60
Traditional agreement, 38
Trust 138

U

Understanding 24
  ambition 24
  desire 24
United front 58, 68

W

Weeks, Dudley Ph.D.
  *The Eight Essential Steps to
    Conflict Resolution* 140
Wegos 20,78
What Mona Lisa Knew, 70
  Mackoff, Dr. Barbara 70
WISE-UP 80
WISH LIST 80
Woman 67
  invisible 67
Women 73
  approachable 73
  attitude 71
  build relationships 75
  caretakers 96
  confidence 73
  conversation. 75
  decision maker 76, 78
  defensive 72
  developing skills 75
  entrepreneur 114
  frustrated 77
  hostility 76
  informed 73
  laughable 71
  lighten up 70
  male, female humor 71
  misunderstood 75
  perspective 71
  relationship building skills
    74
  satisfaction 89
  sense of humor 70

somber 70
start-ups 79
taboo 71
talk 74
watch and wait 79
Working Together
  control 25
  desire 24
  disappointed 26
  dislike business 26
  economical 25
  family life 27, 39
  flexibility 27
  gopher 25
  how 35
  one want to 26
  option 25
  principles 123
  professionalism 26
  reason 27
  resistance 26
  respect abilities 25
  responsibility 25
  share life 25
  sharing 25
  sorry 26
  status 25
  trustworthy partner 25
  unqualified 26
  who wants to 19
  work for free. 25

Y

You Just Don't Understand 75
  Deborah Tannen 75

Video Learning Kit

Couples in Business Together

Through their own experienes, nine couples offer candid advice about how to work together successfully. Three key elements — strategic and shared decision- making, balance and plannng and control — frame this half-hour video and the integrated self-assessment checklist.

Management issues addressed include: building teamwork, defining division of responsibility, positioning for growth, balancing work and home, and extending the notion of family into the workplace. Couples learn from the compelling experiences of other business-owning couples and with the use of a structured guide to evaluate their own situations.

The Austin Family Business Program provides hands-on learning opportunities — workbooks, checklist, videos — to help business-owning families manage day-to-day operations and plan for future generations. Practical lessons, targeted to established family businesses, are offered in a variety of affordable and easily-accessible formats.

———————————————————————————————

To order the video learning kit for $79.00, plus shipping, or request a catalog of products for family businesses, call (800) 859-7609.

For more informatin contact:
Austin Family Business Program
College of Business, Oregon State University
Corvallis, Oregon 97331-2603
(800) 859-7609 P or (541) 737-5388 F
or visit our website at:
http://www.bus.orst.edu/fam_bus/afbphome.htm

Coming Soon!

A new book about couples who live and work the life of their dreams.

Couples at Work
??????????????????????
What Does It Take To Live Your Dreams?
How Can You Have The Perfect Life?
How Can You Live Life On Your Own Terms?

Can you help us with a subtitle? Send us your ideas!

For a limited time, we will be conducting a survey to determine what couples think their dream life is, what prevents them from living it now; or if they are living it, how they achieved it. Let us know if you want to participate in the survey and it will be mailed, faxed or emailed.

We make every effort to maintain the confidentiality of our survey respondents. Those named in this book gave written authorization to publish their quotes and names or initials as well as place of residence.

Boomer House Books, LLC
191 University Blvd., #323
Denver, Colorado 80206-4613
800-994-6203 Fax
email: djj@privatei.com
www.boomer-house-books.com

We WelcomeYour Feedback!

ORDERS SHIPPED SAME DAY AS RECEIVED!

✳   Fax orders: (800) 994-6203

☎   Telephone orders: Call Toll Free: (800) 994-6069

💻   On-line orders: djj@privatei.com or
        Website www.boomer-house-books.com

✍   Postal orders: Boomer House Books, 191 University
        Blvd., Suite 323, Denver, Colorado 80206-4613, USA

Please send the following: I understand that I may return any books for a full refund — for any reason, no questions asked.

Couples at Work: How Can You Stand to Work With Your Spouse?	**Quantity**	**Price** $18.95 ea.	**Total**
	Sales Tax*:		
	Shipping**:		*3.50*
	Total:		

***Colorado** residents add .75 sales tax per book.
**Shipping for the first book is $3.50 and .75 for each additional book.

Payment: ❑ Check or money order
           ❑ Credit card: ❑ VISA   ❑ MC   ❑ AMEX

Card number: _____

Name on card:_____ Exp. Date: / _____

Signature: _____

Send to:

      Name:_____

      Address:_____

      City:_____ State:_____ Zip:_____

      Phone: (   )_____

Call *toll free* and order now!

ORDERS SHIPPED SAME DAY AS RECEIVED!

✳   Fax orders: (800) 994-6203

☎   Telephone orders: Call Toll Free: (800) 994-6069

💻   On-line orders: djj@privatei.com or
       Website www.boomer-house-books.com

✉   Postal orders: Boomer House Books, 191 University
       Blvd., Suite 323, Denver, Colorado 80206-4613, USA

Please send the following: I understand that I may return any
books for a full refund — for any reason, no questions asked.

Couples at Work:	Quantity	Price	Total
How Can You Stand		$18.95 ea.	
to Work With Your	*Sales Tax*:*		
Spouse?	*Shipping**:*		3.50
	Total		

***Colorado** residents add .75sales tax per book.
**Shipping for the first book is $3.50 and .75 for each additional book.

Payment: ❑   Check or money order
           ❑   Credit card: ❑ VISA   ❑ MC   ❑ AMEX

Card number: _____

Name on card: _____ Exp. Date: ___/_____

Signature: _____

Send to:

       Name: _____

       Address: _____

       City: _____ State:___ Zip: _____

       Phone: ( ) _____

           Call *toll free* and order now!